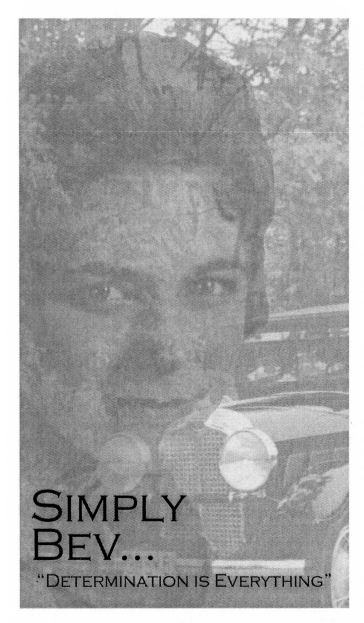

SIMPLY BEV...
"DETERMINATION IS EVERYTHING"

James H. Cox

iUniverse, Inc.
Bloomington

SIMPLY BEV...
"DETERMINATION IS EVERYTYHING"

iUniverse books may be ordered through booksellers or by contacting:

iUniverse
1663 Liberty Drive
Bloomington, IN 47403
www.iuniverse.com
1-800-Authors (1-800-288-4677)

ISBN: 978-1-4502-8222-2 (dj)

Library of Congress Control Number: 2010918871

Printed in the United States of America

iUniverse rev. date: 12/13/2010

This book is dedicated to
the loving memory of Beverly.

4353

bev kimes

girl on the go

Forward

When I made the decision to do this biography, I really didn't know much about Bev's early life, since she didn't discuss it much. She had talked about a few singular points in time, but nothing in detail. I am forever grateful to her; for saving all the things she did save. Without these notebooks full of letters, notes and pictures, this book would not have been possible...at least in the sense that I wanted it to be. Many people knew Beverly from different sectors of her life, but none really knew what drove her determination, quest for knowledge and her need to help people. Others suggested that they would be interested in doing a biography about Beverly that chronicled her career. My interest was in writing about Beverly's life in general, and how she became the person she was.

I met Beverly in 1981, and we were married July 6,1984; three years from the day that we met. We were very well suited for each other, in many different ways. We shared everything: our knowledge, hobbies, our work and our lives ... equally. We were truly partners in everything that we did. We travel extensively by automobile, and visited a lot of historic towns and places, since we both enjoyed history and reliving it as much as we could. Prior to spending our Thanksgiving tradition with our friends, John and Ann, we would always leave New York on Wednesday evening, with an area in mind to visit, but with no particular time schedule. One such trip, had us following the Mason-Dixon trail, thru Delaware and Virginia, and visiting all the Civil War battle grounds, as well Monticello and the University of Virginia. A lot of other similar trips were also taken.

Beverly had a lot of health problems. These, at times, made it more difficult for her to get her work done; but it never stopped her. I knew very well what Bev worked on during the time we were together. In the process of writing this story, however, I was totally in awe at just how much she had done... in all aspects of her life (not only during the 27 years that we were together, but even more so, in the last ten years of her life.)

One thing I wanted, more than anything, was to see Bev recover her health, get back home, and continue her life and work. I guess I knew this wasn't going to be.

I am so happy that we had all the good years together, and that I was there to help her through it all, as much as I could. Although into every life a little rain must fall, I can attest to the fact that the good times with Bev far exceed the bad ones.

It is with much love, admiration and respect that I have dedicated myself to write her story. Beverly deserves her life story to be told, and it's my hope that those who read this book will have better understanding of just who Beverly Rae Kimes really was.

Chapter 1:
The Early Years

Beverly Rae Kimes was born in West Chicago, Illinois, August 17, 1939. She was the daughter of Raymond L. and Grace D. Parrin Kimes. Her middle name, Rae (after her father), would be of some help to her later on in life. She was nicknamed Fuzzy, for her lack of hair at birth...and for sometime after.

Beverly at about 6 months

Ray and Grace were married on November 25, 1937. Grace was a 1936 graduate of the

Ray and Grace circa 1959

Comptometer School, in Chicago. (The comptometer was a machine that was used, at that time, to keep company records for expenditures and sales.) She worked for Sears, Roebuck and Company at their headquarters, in Chicago until early 1939. At that time, pregnant with Beverly, she left her job and was given a glowing letter of recommendation from her boss. Typical of life back then, Grace stayed home to raise the family, and Ray went to work to support them. Grace did not re-enter the work force until the mid sixties, after both daughters were out on their own.

They lived in West Chicago for about two years, in a house with a backyard sandbox. On good days, Bev played in the sandbox. The house was close to the tracks of the Chicago Northwestern Railroad, her father's employer. When some of the trains passed, the engineers who knew Ray — and where he lived — would honk the train horn as a "hello" to Bev as she played.

Knowing that this was really not a desirable neighborhood for the family, and particularly for Bev, they started looking for other places to live. At the time, the search was somewhat hampered by Ray's earnings as a "fireman" for Chicago North Western. (His job was to shovel coal into the firebox of the locomotive.) The house search, however, would soon be changed by a stroke of good luck and Grace's brother, Howard, who was planning to relocate to California.

Since Howard and his wife, Vern, wanted to leave as soon as possible, a deal was struck between the two families. Howard and Vern packed up their things, and their two children, Jacquie and Bruce, and headed west. The Kimes family happily moved into Howard and Vern's

515 South Hale Street

former home at 515 South Hale Street. Once in California, Howard and Vern never returned to Wheaton for visits. (In later years, Bev did go to visit them; I accompanied her on a visit in the mid-eighties, which was the last time that she would make the trip.)

The house was sold as a "kit" through the Sears, Roebuck catalog (In the early 1900's, a vast array of things were sold this way; for example, the Sears Motor Buggy, a horseless carriage that Beverly would own later in her life.) There was a lot of painting and fixing that was needed to make the house a home. At the time, Ray was gone for days on runs with the railroad. While away, he sent many letters to Grace pleading with her not to work too hard and wait for him to return and help. In one letter, Ray said that due to lack of man power, he would be away a few days longer than expected; but this was good, because

Ray at the controls

he was being paid $10.00 a day. As he put it, they "sure could use the extra money." In all his letters, he always asked, about "Snooky Pants," a nickname for Bev — but only used by him.

The repairs to the house were completed in a short time, and the family settled in for what would be a long time — 1942 to 1982. This was the only house that Bev lived in, until she went off to college in the Fall of 1957. Ray and Grace would continue to live there, until after his retirement from the   railroad. Ray was an engineer at the time of his retirement and for many years prior. The reason he retired, as he put it, "I was just fed up with these new whippersnapper's telling me how to run my train." Ray and Grace retired to Eagle River, Wisconsin in 1982.

In the late 80's, Bev and I were out West on a summer vacation and, at Bev's request, we went to see 515. (The number was the only thing needed for the family to refer to their home.) There was a woman working outside, and Beverly got out of the car and approached her. As it turned out, she was quite friendly, and invited Bev and I inside to show Bev all the things that she and her husband had been doing to restore the house. They wanted it to appear as original as they could, as it has been back in the 1920's. This was a very happy day for Bev; not only did she get to revisit her childhood home, she also learned that someone caring now owned and lived at 515.

In March of 1942, Bev's sister, Sharon, was born; her nickname was "Muscles." In their early years, the girls didn't have too much in common. Sharon was a "tom boy," through and through. She preferred cars, trucks and toy gas stations. Beverly preferred dolls and other girly things.

Father, Beverly and Sharon-Circa, late 1940's

On one occasion, Bev had just finished curtseying and seating her paper dolls, when Sharon snuck up

3

from behind and blew them all down. To get even, Bev cut the strings on the car elevator of Sharon's service station.

Bev's favorite doll, Sparkle Plenty, which underwent many repairs by her father, was finally retired when she turned thirteen. The doll, along with many other childhood memories, were stored away in boxes and remained there till her death.

One of the favorite things for Bev, Sharon and their friends, were the ball games that they played in the back lot behind the house. Bev's father would do the pitching; her mom was the umpire. (There were many of these games when her father could be at home.)

There were summer vacation trips, during her growing-up years to various lakes: such as Lake Geneva in Illinois, or Lake Okauchee in Wisconsin. Bev made a footnote in her scrapbook, that said: "These visits were sexual summers, and always fun." By "sexual," Bev

referred to interaction with boys, as in "flirting"; not to be interpreted as having sex. (Things were much different, in terms of meaning, back then.) They went to Lake Tomahawk, in Wisconsin, which Bev said, "...was no fun and left a lot to be desired."

Bev, Sharon and their dad at the lake, circa 1955

On alternate vacation trips, Bev and Sharon would be allowed to take turns bringing a friend. Whenever Bev had a friend for the trip, they would pick on Sharon, until she moaned and complained to the point that she would have to be moved to the front seat, between her parents. Then, all was good in the back seat.

Bev spent one week in Minocqua, Wisconsin, with her friend, Myra Darrow and Myra's dad. On this trip, according to her diary, Bev appointed herself "Chief of Research Department of 'Dreamboats' (exceptionally good looking boys)." She also made some trips to Williams Bay and Crystal Lake with her friend, Janet Heitzler and

4

Janet's father.

All in all, Beverly and her family did have a lot of fun vacations. On one occasion, while Bev, Sharon and Janet were swimming in the lake, they decided to skinny dip. They removed and tied their bathing suits to the swimming dock, and when it was time to get out of the water, Sharon's suit was missing. (It seems that it had mysteriously floated away!) Sharon wouldn't come out of the water until dark. This incident did not amuse their mother — and having to buy another swimming suit — didn't either. The three-year age difference made Sharon, most often, the brunt of the pranks (which is understandable during their early years). This changed in their later years, however, and their relationship became very close.

The family's means of transportation in the early years, was an old 1937 Pontiac (which finally gave way to a Kaiser, in the early 50's.) This was the car that Beverly drove to take her driver's test for her license in 1956. It was also the one and only car in which she was involved in an accident. While stopping at the local gas station, she, "...gently motored into the gas pump."

In all, Bev didn't drive very much, until she arrived at Penn State and had to make her rounds to theaters. Later, when she arrived in New York City, her driving pretty much ceased, except for an occasional rental. She once told me, "Once, I was returning from the Hershey Pennsylvania Antique Car Meet, and made my way back to New York City by way of Philadelphia; I am a little geographically challenged." When we first met, she confessed, "I have a driver's license for identification purposes only, and I make a very good passenger. So, why should I drive?"

Sharon's wedding (L-R)
Bridesmaid, Carol Brazzale,
Sharon, Tom and Beverly

The Kaiser was replaced with a 1955 Ford Fairlane, in the late 50's. It was a turquoise and white color combination. A speedboat, built by Ray and son-in-law, Tom Sauer, was added. (Tom and Sharon had married in October 1959.) The speedboat added a lot more fun to the lake vacations; with boating, water skiing, and tubing.

One of many stories told about Bev's early years, was about a pet named, Sally Ann. Sally Ann was a chicken. When she was not around on a particular Sunday, Bev and Sharon were quite concerned, especially when Sunday dinner turned out to be chicken. Beverly asked her Mom, "This is not Sally Ann, is it Mom?" Her mother assured her that it was not, and that Sally Ann must have wandered off, and would most likely come back.

That night, Ray and Grace went out to a chicken farm to look for a replacement (which took quite some doing.) Eventually, they did find one that would pass as Sally Ann. The next morning, the girls discovered that their beloved chicken had returned home. Needless to say "new" Sally Ann died of old age. (The real truth came many years later.)

Another fond memory from Bev's diary: "One evening, Sharon and I went uptown to sell Christmas cards and had taken our dog, Tuffy, along with us. We were so overwhelmed with our success, that we returned home, leaving Tuffy tied to a parking meter." A speedy retreat was made to retrieve Tuffy, and thankfully, he was still tied to the meter.

Sharon, Tuffy and Beverly, circa 1955

Bev had attached the following note to a greeting card, sent about 1962, when she must have been away at college: "From Mr. Harry Chartterton of Wheaton — a kindly white-haired gentleman who never forgets a birthday, special occasion or any holiday. As a child, I used to sit hours with him, chatting and drinking Welch's grape juice."

Beverly was also in the Girl Scouts for a while. (I'm not sure exactly how long.) She told me that the reason

6

she gave it up was, "I didn't like digging the trenches, much less using them."

Bev's caption, "Here I am at the Lagoon, looking beautiful".

One of Bev's favorite places to hang out in her teenage years, was the Lagoon, where she spent many happy hours. As she said in her scrapbook, "My two favorite things: skating and Pete Rolher." (Pete was her first puppy love.) In a later note, when she was in early high school, she said, "Dances. I dreaded and avoided them as much as possible, and dated as little as social connotations allowed; instead, I entered into a dream world, in which my romantic interest could not be filled by any high school boy."

Do not let these statements lead you to think that this girl was not popular, well liked and respected by her classmates and friends. Quite the contrary; as could be attested to by all the notes and well wishes from the teachers and students signing her yearbooks.

Bev at one of those dreaded dances, in the early 50's

Beverly spent a lot of her teenage years babysitting, as did most female teenagers at this time. It was a good way to earn spending money, and the demand for this service was high. As she stated, "I spent a good deal of my time babysitting, not primarily because of maternal instincts, but because I liked the money."

During her high school years, Bev worked part-time at the Wheaton Theater. She spent "many hysterical hours" there as cashier or candy girl. "One of the best perks, was getting to see the movies without having to pay."

Like most teenage girls at the time, she had an all-consuming crush on James Dean. "Myra, Bonnie and I held séances to try to contact him. Cindy was a cynic; needless to say, no luck." Another one of her movie idols was Marlon Brando. She said, "I saw *On The Water Front* eight times and knew the dialogue by heart; and wrote it all down."

Other idols were General MacArthur and Nellie Fox of the White Sox. Bev attended quite a few of the White Sox games with her Mom and Aunt Olive. She saved a Jr. White Sox fan pennant (with a fan button attached), as well as three White Sox annuals with all the team's signature's on the back. Her note attached to the pennant said, " A White Sox fan forever, or as long as it takes." Beverly attached notes to everything she saved, including, "First prize that I ever won, for Pin the Tail on the Donkey, in February of 1945."

The Kimes family was Catholic; so both Beverly and Sharon would spend their first six years learning at Saint Michael's School in Wheaton, which was about two blocks behind their house. I don't have much information about these years. I can only assume that Bev did well there,

because I found an Honor Certificate awarded to Beverly for having an excellent record of attendance and punctuality, dated June 9, 1947; signed by Sister M. Thonetta. One thing I do know, Bev told me both girls were very happy to move on to the public schools. Beverly entered Wheaton Jr. High in the Fall of 1951.

Bev and her dad,
Confirmation Day

In 1952, Bev debuted in her first play, *Why the Chimes Rang*. She saved the script, and wrote on it: "My theatrical debut as a star, 8th grade Christmas Play. Had 102 lines. Everyone said I was great." In 1956, she appeared in the play, *Gramercy Ghost,* and wrote: "Had a small part, wasn't particularly impressing, but had a wonderful time."

In the late eighties, she had a brief appearance on a Broadway stage, in the play *Dame Edna;* she was summoned from the audience, by Dame Edna, to participate in a small skit.

8

In1956, in her junior year, she wrote a term paper, *Statehood for Alaska and Hawaii*. She was given an 'A', but more poignant, were the comments of the teacher on the front of the term paper: "Outstanding level of research." He asked to keep the paper to be used as an example for future classes. In the future, Bev's skills in research and writing would make her the most respected author in her field, and earn her many awards of recognition for her work.

In her high school years, Bev joined the National Thespian Society and the National Honor Society for Secondary Schools. In addition to her required studies, she was also involved in the GAA Club, and lettered in bowling. She said, "I wasn't an outstanding athlete, just persistent."

As for speech and choir, "...often corny but fun." The Fortune Guild: "My favorite. My beginning of interest in the theater."

She was also involved in: the Pep Club, Thespians, Library Assistant, Glee Club, F.T.A, Treasurer, Usher Club, Poetry Club, Dog Club, Student Court and *Wecomi* (the student newspaper).

At her graduation ceremony, she was seated in the first two rows, reserved for the "Brains and Brawn Masses" (as described by fellow student, Jerry Kissel.) She graduated with honors, held straight A's, made honor roll, received two gold stars from the National Thespians, and 100-point gold activity pin and 50 point silver activity pin from the National Honor Society.

After graduation, in her scrapbook along with her graduation papers and graduation photograph, she wrote: "Despite honors received, I never looked on my high school years as successful. I never hit the top.

Bev in her graduation gown

9

I was secretary, treasurer, had a small part, was a member, but I never lead, or had the lead; I look forward to college for these goals."

A famous quote says "Some succeed because they are destined to, but most succeed because they are determined to." Beverly certainly was determined. In her junior year of college, she made a caricature of a female on the run, with a caption of "Beverly, girl on the go." Using this, she would make personalized note pads for herself. She just refused to settle for good. Only the best would satisfy her to meet the goals she had set for herself at the conclusion of high school.

In the future, Beverly would attain many goals; in 2005 she received, a lifetime Achievement Award from IAMA, a Society that judges the works of automobile writers and authors. The society annually held banquets at Sardi's Restaurant in New York City, to honor and present awards to the winners. The I.A.M.A (International Automotive Media Awards) Society, was spearheaded by Walter and Elaine Hassner of Tucson, Arizona. They owned Aztex Corporation, which published. *Rene Dreyfus, Biography, My Two Lives,* as well as many other books on automotive subjects.

Walter Hassner, presenting an award to Bev, for Best Magazine, 2002

Before going off to college, Bev would take a summer job with Sears, Roebuck and Company at their Chicago headquarters. She worked as a "fill-in" for personnel taking vacations. Her first summer, she served as private secretary to Mr. H.A. Alexander, Dept 637. She would return each summer, until she graduated from the University of Illinois, and headed east for Penn State University, at State College, Pa., for her Master's degree.

At some point in the summer, before going off to college, Bev told me, "My friend, Myra, and I were out on a nice summer evening driving around in Myra's new

Plymouth convertible..." (a graduation present from her father), when the girls came up with an idea to pull a caper. Driving to the outskirts of Wheaton, they pulled into

the parking lot of Mike's General Store. Myra stayed in the car with the motor running, and Bev went inside. She snatched a pack of Hostess Twinkies, ran back to the car, and they made their get-away. Fortunately, no consequence followed this act; but she kept those Twinkies, maybe as a reminder, but to my knowlege, nothing like that ever happened again.

The actual Hostess Twinkies, after 53 years of storage.

There were many people who influenced Bev, in addition to her parents. Her maternal grandmother, Anna Perrin, was abandoned by her husband in the 1920's. He left her to raise eight children by herself. In order to do this, Anna took in laundry and did other chores to provide for herself and the children. She also did a lot of canning of vegetables and fruits, which helped to hold down the cost of food. Beverly and Sharon both spent considerable time with

Anna Perrin, Bev's maternal grandmother

their grandmother. After a bad fall and a broken hip in her later years, Anna was confined to the Parkway Nursing Home in Wheaton. She never lost her faculties, and stayed in constant touch with Beverly by cards and letters. She was of sound mind until she passed away at the age of 104. I have to believe that her gusto rubbed off on Beverly.

Bev was also influenced by her Aunt Olive, Grace's sister; Uncle Charles (Rudy) Vogel, who encouraged her relentlessly; and Grace's other sister, Aunt Freida and Uncle Charlie Woodruff, who were her godparents. Letters from all of them included constant pleas of "Take care of yourself, and don't overdo it." This was, in part, due to Bev's medical issues, which I will address later in this book.

Olive and Charles Vogel (in Conductor's hat) at Chicago Train Station

In her childhood, Bev also knew a person who she called, Uncle Kenny. She learned later, that Uncle Kenny was actually her half-brother; a son of Ray's from a previous marriage. That young relationship later rekindled around the late 1990's. Kenny and wife, Dorothy, were in a time-share program and came to East Bushkill, Pennsylvania. Bev and I spent a week with them, along with Sharon and her husband, Herb. From that point on, the relationship blossomed, until Ken Passed away. From this renewal, came new relatives, Kenneth L. Jr., Kathryn C, Kristine A. and Karen Rae.

In 1999, Kenneth's daughter, Kathy, came to New York, with her daughter, Jenna, and a group that was going to perform in concert at Carnegie Hall. We set up a dinner meeting with the whole group at B.B.Q. (a restaurant on Third Avenue by 77th Street). This turned out to be quite a "hoot", as each child was responsible for his or her own food tab. Some children had cash, some had credit cards. Needless to say, it was a fiasco for the waiter; so I offered to pay the tab with my credit card. Kathy agreed to reimburse me later, when she was able to get all the funds in order. It was also quite a bit of fun to redirect them to their buses back to their hotel. We attended the Concert, and it was really quite good. Imagine, kids from Arkansas making a hit on stage at Carnegie Hall; a lifetime memory, to be sure.

L-R: Howard (Doc) Perrin, Charlie and Frieda Woodruff, and Vern

L-R: Bev and mel, Ken, Herb, and Sharon

12

Chapter 2:
University of Illinois,
Urbana, Illinois

Freshman year, Beverly chose the Theta Upsilon Sorority. There were several letters sent to her prior to her leaving Wheaton to go the university. They welcomed her, saying that the staff was looking forward to her arrival. They confirmed that she had made a good choice, and would be joining a nice group of women.

Bev started to get involved right away as a freshman manager, and later as a sophomore manager, for the *Illio*, (the university's annual year book). Bev was a Alpha Lam Scholarship honorary, and served on the committee of the 38th annual Dad's Day weekend — a yearly activity to honor fathers and students. She also entered the Dolphin Queen contest, although I have no information on

the results. She said, "...found out about the Standard Board (the hard way). Came in late, and was fined." There was also an occasion, when she was also cited for being too loud in the shower.

Beverly and date, Joe Schauer, Christmas dance,1958

Beverly was head of entertainment for The Annual Mother's Day Banquet. She also became a crew member of the University Theater. This pretty much sums up her freshman year. Starting this year, and through her senior year, she kept scrapbooks; a total of eight. These scrapbooks are the source of the information about Bev's early years that is included in this biography.

13

As a University of Illinois sophomore in 1958, Bev was elected to Shi-Ai, a Sophomore Woman's Honorary Sorority. Members were chosen from freshmen who were outstanding in scholarship and activities. A note in her scrapbook says: "My most rewarding experience. I walked in the Honor's Day Procession and was introduced at the Shi Ai sing, which is an annual event on Mother's Day Weekend."

Beverly and her mom,
Mothers Day, at U.of I.,
1960

She was a member of the University Theater, a sophomore assistant and junior department manager in charge of properties, staging, and construction. Ultimately, she was appointed General Manager.

She ran for Student Senate, district 7. "My Campaign Slogan: Keep Up With The Times, Vote For Kimes." In her scrapbook she wrote, "Although I lost the election by only five votes, the experience far outweighed the disappointment."

She was also a Rush Hostess. A Rush Hostess was assigned to take the rushes (freshman) through the sorority houses, so that they could make a choice of which one they wanted to join. This was not an easy task, since it was a tight time schedule, and often required taking taxies to meet the timeframe.

She was also leader of the Freshman Exchange. The purpose of the Exchange, was to acquaint various groups of freshman women with the campus; which, she is quoted as saying was, "very successful." A note from her pledge Mother, Shirley Ashton, read: "Dear Bev, May you always remember this day as one of your happiest experiences in Theta Upsilon, college and life."

14

Later, she served as Rush Chairman, Sheequon Chairman and Editor. Bev was also in charge of the initiation skit for the incoming freshmen, and head of the skit for the Acacia Exchange, "It was hysterical." She was Dining Room Chairman for the Mardi Gras Dance, and head of entertainment for the Mother's Day Dance.

She was also assistant manager of Star Course, the University's Concert and Entertainment Board. "I spent most of my time in workshops. I loved it; every minute of it. Theater is wonderful." She also served as recording secretary for meetings and editor for their publication, *Star Dust*.

She was elected Editor of the Gamma Chapter of the Upsilon National Social Sorority. "I wrote all the newspaper articles and Dial Reports (Dial is a National Magazine for the arts) in my capacity as editor. I loved it. It was also was helpful to in my journalism training." A Gamma Chapter article about Beverly appears in the appendix of this book.

Early in1961, she wrote an article titled, *Props,* for *Dial Magazine, Dramatics, an Educational Magazine for Directors, Teachers and Students of Dramatic Arts.* It was published in January of 1962; her first time being published. She was paid $25.00. In a letter to her from the editor, Leon C. Miller, he said in closing, "Thank you for submitting the article. I feel it has much to offer to our over 2200+ affiliated schools."

January 3,1959. A bad turn of events. She writes: "That ****** kidney! I was stricken with nephritis. It was a frightening experience, but it showed me how many friends I had. I received over 200 cards and many letters and gifts from well wishers."

Beverly took a leave of absence from college

15

and went home for her convalescence, which was mostly rest and relaxation. She was taking only one medication, and was treated by the family doctor, Dr. Dan D. Jamison, of the Medical and Dental Center in Wheaton. In a letter dated February 5,1959, written to Beverly, he said, "A test taken on the specimen the day you left to go back to college showed a slight disturbance that you should report to the clinic; a report is enclosed, which you may present as

Beverly at home
convalescing, 1959

evidence; plus take with you an early morning specimen."

"That ***** kidney" would be an ongoing problem for Bev for the rest of her life. I found records of other visits to other doctors and hospitals for this problem up into the 1960's.

When she returned to school, Bev wrote: "Early Spring. As part of the Illini Union, I was property chairman for the spring musical, *Oklahoma*. It was an experience that I'll never forget. Getting a surrey was a problem, and not the only one. What a riot."

Headlines in the newspaper read: "Performance of Entire Cast, Makes Oklahoma a Success." Bev's note in the scrapbook, "...the result of a lot of work – an almost professional show. Just like Broadway. I later became a Major Chairman of The Illini Union Board."

Mask and Bauble, a theater honor organization, initiated 20 pledges. Bev's note: "Mask and Bauble Theater Honorary. I was so happy that I was chosen. Also appointed House Rush Chairman of Theta Upsilon Social Sorority... an honor and a lot of hard work."

"I entered a Spring Speech Contest. One of six finalists. What an experience. Originally, there were 300 students entered in the contest. The six

16

finalists spoke in Latzer Hall. My subject...what do you think? My personal favorite, Capital Punishment. Was I scared? Was I!!! Awarded The Alfred D. Houston Memorial Award in public speaking; for participation in the final round, which symbolizes excellence in public speaking." This was a contest done every year, in honor of a distinguished Alfred D. Houston alum.

In later years, Bev became a wizard at narrating at automobile Concours, and as a guest speaker at many Car Club meetings.

Her favorite story, which she told many audiences, (including the Westfall Township, Pennsylvania D.V.R. 7th grade students), was "*What If?*" It's was a story of a transcontinental trip in a 1903 Winton, from San Francisco to New

Beverly, Concoures of The Eastern United States, June 2002

York. The trip was made by Dr. H. Nelson Jackson and his mechanic, S. K. Crocker. They departed from San Francisco on May 23, 1903, and arrived in New York City on July 26. It is quite a story; Can you imagine almost two months to make a trip, that now could be done easily in four days? For those who are curious, I have included a copy of this entire story in the appendix of this book.

Bev received ten notes of thanks from the D.V.R students. One of these read: "Dear Miss Kimes, I really had fun listening about cars, and what the world is like with them and would be without them. They are very interesting to hear about, and the styles are really far out. My father and I both enjoy your books, so please keep writing. Thank You, Greg Grigas."

Bev became a member of the university film council, chair for cinema international, and was the recording secretary as well. Her job was to procure foreign films to be shown on campus. This was not an

17

easy task, since it required a lot of time and correspondence to get films. She also became a member of Illini Forum of the Forensic Association, a weekly radio program where current and contemporary subjects of interest are discussed by students.

At the beginning of her Junior year, (1959–60), Bev placed a typed sheet titled "My Prayer" on the front cover of her scrapbook number five:

"Lord, Thou knowest better than I know myself, that I am growing older; and, as such, should act grown-up. Keep me from getting talkative, and particularly from the fatal habit of thinking I must say something on every subject and on every occasion. Release me from my craving to try to straighten out everybody's affairs. Keep my mind free from the recital of endless details. Give me wings to get to the point. I ask for grace enough to listen to the tales of other's pains. Help me to endure them with patience. But seal my lips on my own aches and pains. They are increasing, and my love of rehearsing them is becoming sweeter.

Teach me the glorious lesson that, occasionally it is possible that I may be mistaken. Help me develop tenacity — let me hold control over my temper, my emotions and my tongue. Make me steadfast — a mind once made up, is made up. Keep me reasonably sweet; I do not want to be a saint — but a sour woman is one of the crowning works of the devil.

Make me thoughtful, but not moody; helpful but not bossy. With my vast store of wisdom, it seems a pity not to use it all — but Thou knowest, Lord, that I want a few friends at the end."

That year, back at University of Illinois, she wrote: "The work of college — school type work, of course; I entered the School of Journalism curriculum

18

in News — Editorial.
Typography class is a real 'killer'
of a course; fun tho."

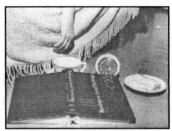

Beverly earned a
reputation on campus as being
the "girl on the go." An article
written by a member of the
Gamma Chapter, listing Bev's
many university achievements
is included in the appendix of
this book.

*Bev's caption, "What we must go
through to get a college degree!"*

A note about the cartoon on her note pads,
(*Bev Kimes, Girl on the Go*). "My finest artistic
achievement: Memo pads, product of Typography
Lab." A memo from the desk of Glen Hanson, her
professor, said the following about this project:
"Design: An amusing cartoon with a good type
choice. The layout is most effective because of the
startling and offbeat of the cut. Production: Pretty
good press work. A bit too much packing on part
of the type, and some of the brush lacks a perfectly
sharp impression." Her grade, over all, was an 'A'.

A note from Professor Brown, (her advisor),
from Bev's Journalism 215 course read: "Miss Kimes,
Your reports were excellent — both quantity and
quality. It was a real pleasure to read them — and I
like those personalized bits, such as Miniver Cheevy
and Payola. Keep Up The Good Work."

"Beginning Reporting, and dear old Mr.
Smith," Bev wrote. "I began to wonder if I could
ever write." From three reports that she wrote, she
received a "Quite Nice," — she   got an 'A'; on the
second, (untitled), "Pretty good intentions, although I
think you're over exuberant." — no grade; and lastly,
The Ideal — she got a 'B'.

More from Bev's notes:
"Our football season: The Fighting Illini. I

attended most games. When the U. of I. played Army; had a date with a Cadet. We corresponded a while, but absence, doesn't make the heart grow fonder."

"I became a member of N.C.P. — a very great honor; I was very, very surprised."

A card from Players Magazine, read: "Dear Miss Kimes, Congratulations, upon your initiation into National Collegiate Players Fraternity."

A card from Linda Bond, Secretary of N.C.P read: "You will be initiated into the National Collegiate Players on January 17, at 4pm, at the 6th Street Building. A smorgasbord dinner will be held at Union, immediately following."

Bev worked, again, in the Theatre Workshop; she did eight plays for the season: *The North Room, The Brothers, The Hot Iron, The Private Life Of The Master Race, The Adding Machine, The Land Of Hearts Desire, The Chairs,* and *Cuthbert Bound.* Bev's note: "Notes from workshop directors not always pleasant, until after opening night."

Beverly and crew — theater workshop

Two headlines from the newspapers, of the play, *Cuthbert Bound* and *Private Life:* "Newton Play Cited as Best. Theatre workshop varied; Sensitive Performances of Leads, Makes *Private Life* Top Production."

Beverly checking props for a play

Also from her notes: "One of the most bizarre props, that I ever had to get was for *Private Life:* a caricature of Hitler, which had to be framed and hung

20

on a wall." Someone did a charcoal drawing for her and saved the day.

"The Illini Union. I became a major chairman of Cinema International." Cinema International is dedicated to showing foreign films of high caliber, to add to the enjoyment and cultural learning of University of Illinois students. Procuring the films was not an easy task. Bev said, "It was very hectic — but, very rewarding — especially when films were well received and well attended."

In the first semester, there were 14 films shown: *The Forty-First* (Russian); *Tales Of Hoffman* (British); *Gervaise* (French); *Pather Panchali* (Indian); *Keeper Of The Night* (German); *The Idiot* (French); *White Reindeer* (Finnish); *Erioca* (German); *La Strada* (Italian); *Samurai* (Japanese); *Bull Fight* (Mexican); *Ordet* (Danish); *The Last Waltz* (Austrian); and *Chandra* (Indian).

These films were shown, from September 20, 1959, thru January 17, 1960. Bev wrote: "Publicity was very good. Press very co-operative; but why did they always quote me?"

Some of these quotes included: "To call the *White Reindeer*, a horror film, might seem to detract from its aesthetic qualities; but, whatever its intent, the result certainly is spine-chilling suspense, says Bev Kimes of Cinema International."

"The *Forty First* was awarded the prize for Best Scenario at the Cannes International Film Festival; in color, this film is considered to be the most beautiful film produced, says Cinema International Chairman, Bev Kimes."

"Since last spring many precautions have been taken by the new major chair to insure Cinema International fans that make their weekly trips to the auditorium, will not be in vain."

21

In a letter, Director, Kay Lash, wrote, "I have been hearing reports of the beautiful job you are doing with Cinema International. Your executive meetings are handled exactly as a committee meeting should be; and in so doing this, you have gained the respect of your chairmen and those working with you. Congratulations, on a fine job thus far, Bev; keep up the good work. I'm expecting big things of you."

A note from Don Welch, (who Bev referred to occasionally as God, ye old President of the Illini Union), read: "In reference to Cinema International. I stopped by, and was thrilled to see the University auditorium crowded. I have so many committees, I really don't have time to stop by much; but, I have heard nothing but fine reports from Bill Yontz and Kay Lash, and thus, I don't feel I need to concern myself."

The following was a headline and article in the local newspaper: "Illini Forum Panel Discusses Effects of Khrushchev's Visit" The discussion was aired on WILL radio. It concerned what had been the effects of Nikita Khrushchev's visit on the American people, the Russian people, and Khrushchev, himself. The panel consisted of: Miss Barbara Gaul, Junior, LAS, and chairman of the radio and television group; Beverly Kimes, Junior, LAS; Dennis Hall, Junior, engineering. The moderator was Hugh Munro, adviser of the Illini Forum. Of the experience, Bev said, "I loved informal discussions, and felt uninhibited. "

Beverly became a member of Torch, a junior woman's activity; and Theta Sigma Phi, a national women's journalism honor society. A letter from Linnea Pearson, dated October 3, 1959, read: "As president of the local chapter of Theta Sigma Phi, national professional fraternity for women in journalism, I have the pleasant duty of informing you that you have met the high scholastic

22

requirements of the Pi chapter. As you may know,
Theta Sigma Phi is a professional organization,
established for the recognition and encouragement
of high scholarship among women in recognized
schools and departments of journalism throughout
the country. You are invited to attend a rushing
breakfast, Sunday, October 11, at 8:30 a.m., in the
Gothic Room at the Illini Union. I hope you can
be with us at that time. Please except my sincere
congratulations. Cordially Yours, Linnea Pearson.
President"

More of Bev's notes:
"Time out. I attended my sister's wedding,
Sharon Ann Kimes, to Thomas Lee Sauer, on Saturday
the 17th of October, 1959. It was a lovely wedding."
Beverly was Sharon's maid of honor, and she said, "It
was a lovely wedding."

Sharon and Tom spent their honeymoon in
New England. There were two children from this
marriage: Cullen T., and Pamela L. From their birth,
until Beverly passed away, she always
doted on them. They especially
looked forward to Christmas time, in
their younger years, when Bev would
be home for the holidays. They always
looked forward to seeing her, and
what great gifts she had for them.

*Pamela and Cullen,
Christmas, early 70's*

Sometime around November
of 1959 (according to Bev's notes), "Was hospital
bound again — dear old McKinley." (McKinley was
the name of the hospital.) I often felt as a permanent
guest." There were dried flowers in the scrapbook,
with a note from Pat Nicklas. She was Bev's pledge
daughter. The note read: " Cheer up Mom, you still
got me!"

Another note from the scrapbooks:
"John McCauley and I renewed an old
romance (freshman year). He did rekindle my interest

23

in fine music, but the romance was short lived."
Contrary to her high school days, Bev seems to have
dated a lot more in college, and did attend a lot
more dances.

This is a funny note that I found:
"They tried to tell me that I enlisted in the
Marines — all I did was send in a post card, (no
obligation), for information; I just liked to receive mail.
A captain from Chanute kept phoning. Poor man,
never did get hold of me; pity."

Among five pages of her scrapbook number
6, (at the start of the second semester of 1960), were
telegrams, greeting cards, written notes and press
releases. These also included some of Bev's
hand-written notes: "My happiest day —
February 19, 1960. I was selected as
General Manager of University Theatre;
I had reached the top."

A note card from Saint Jude,
Chicago read: Dear Client of Saint Jude:
I have received your request for prayers
at the Nation's Shrine of Saint Jude,
and you can be certain of our faithful
remembrance in the Masses and novena
devotions at the Shrine. The Dominican

*Beverly in her office
as General Manager
of University Theater*

Fathers welcome the opportunity to pray for your
intentions, and thank you most sincerely, for your help
in their important works of aiding worthycandidates
for the priesthood, and in promoting devotion to
Saint Jude.

Bev's note regarding Saint Jude read: "I
asked for the help of St Jude, before petitioning to
the saints of hopeless cases, and to God. I prayed for
the position I wanted more than anything else; the
position I thought I would never get; the position for
which I was subsequently chosen: General Manager."

Bev, as General Manager, and her staff combined work and fun with pizza-paint parties and production parties. "As member of the Board, I was invited to Cam Gullette's home, a faculty rep on the board. It was a short get-together with all board members. It was delightful; I even dank coffee, and enjoyed it! I felt important, and it was a rewarding experience."

Later, she stepped down. "I have finished my work at Illini Union — I left in good graces." A letter from Gretchen Myers read: "I am so happy that you'll be the Cinema International Major Chairman. I have a hunch that this program will boom with you at the helm."

Board members of the
University Theatre

A letter from Ettabelle Schwartz, read: "You organized and led the committee so efficiently. I felt that I never had Cinema International as one of my committees, because I didn't have to be checking up on it at all. Your work in the Illini Union has left its impressions, and has honored you in the building and advancement of an area covered by the committee you head. I admire and appreciate your deep interest and devotion," Bev said, "I enjoyed being chairman; it brought me a love of foreign films, which I'm sure I'll never lose."

More of Bev's notes from other honors:
My 2nd biggest day — I was tapped for Mortar Board, women's highest activity honorary." The following is a telegram from the Mortar Board, National Senior Women's Scholastic Activity Honorary, and Champaign Urbana Alumnae. "Congratulations, on being tapped for Mortar Board; we are proud." There was a reception tea given in honor of her outstanding service in activities.

Bev also received the following invitation from the Newman Club: "Newman Club cordially invites

25

you, in   recognition of your outstanding leadership
and service as a Catholic student in campus
activities, to the First Annual Recognition Tea, Sunday
May 22nd, 1960." A note from Bev read:
" Scholarship and my academic life —
yes, I did have some time for studies."

An article in the press read: "Dean's List.
Beverly Rae Kimes, 515 S. Hale St Wheaton, has been
named to the Dean's List of the University of Illinois,
College of Journalism and Communication for high
scholarship. Miss Kimes maintained an average of
4.19, out of a possible 5.0 for the spring semester.
She was awarded a $100.00 scholarship"

During her senior year (September 1960 to
June 1961),   Beverly was 21, and old enough to vote
for the first time. "It didn't take me long to pick my
candidate, John F. Kennedy." She was a card carrier
for the University of Illinois Young Democrats and Illini
for Kennedy groups. "I was a rather passive member
of the Young Democrats. I did help with canvassing
of voters and with writing papers giving Kennedy's
views, experience, etc. I'm not the button,
poster-waving type, but I did."

"Senator Kennedy visited the campus,
October 24, 1960. The crowd was compared to those
famed water fight mobs. The Senator gave a striking
speech, despite behavior of an enthusiastic crowd."

"My first Election; as a student, I had to vote
absentee ballot. This did not dampen, at all, my
enthusiasm in being able to vote for the first time."
Beverly remained a steadfast Democrat for the
rest of her life.

In a letter from the 1961 *Illio* (Student YearBook):
"Dear Campus Leader,
Due to your position in campus activities,
you have been selected to have your photograph
appear in the 'Who's Who' section of the *Illio* of

1961." Bev was also in photos in seven more entries in the year book.

December 1960. "Back in the hospital again; this time, a new one, University of Illinois Research Hospital, in Chicago. Was a thrilling experience, I had a biopsy taken or done or whatever you do with a biopsy."

Notes from her scrap book, around December of 1960:
"I begin to worry about the future — soon, I'll be leaving the protective wing of the University; What then? I'm thinking of grad school, newspaper work, magazine work — a lot of things."

Former bosses from Sears offered to write recommendations for her; the Air Force sent an invitation for her to join the Officers Training School; and she applied to the C.I.A. "Mr. Gage was charming and impressed; unfortunately my health intervened. I'm wondering what will be best for me. So, I go back to my good friend St Jude."

"I continue as General Manager of The University Theatre, and I created my first Theatre Booklet. My first journalistic endeavor; I wrote the copy and did the layout. It was a very lauded booklet — I was very happy and a bit proud. The University Theatre sponsored the Cleveland Playhouse production of The *Tragic History of Doctor Faustus*, a tremendous success. I was the Hostess at a informal party for the cast, afterward. They were wonderful. Richard Halverson was fascinating. What a General Manager does — everything generally. I was asked to serve as a judge for the Illini Union Campus Talent Auditions and served as Board Secretary; I began preparing for the new staff that will take my place."

First semester of senior year was coming to a close. Bev wrote, "When I have nothing else to do, of course, I played the role of student."

27

A press release in the Wheaton paper read: "Honor Student, Beverly Rae Kimes, 515 S. Hale Street, Wheaton, is among students recognized for superior scholarship in the fall semester by the University of Illinois, College of Journalism and Communications.

A letter from the Dean, J H. Schacht to Bev's dad, read: "Dear Mr. Kimes, It is a pleasure to inform you that your daughter, Beverly, was outstanding in her studies this past semester in the school of journalism and communications. She made a grade of 4.33 out of a possible 5.0 for the semester. Congratulations, to both you and Beverly, for her fine record. Cordially, J H. Schacht." Bev's note attached to this document, read: "What do you think you are — Kimes? Intelligent or something?."

The following are notes from her last semester, senior year:
"I register for the last time at the old U. of I. Only 246 days until graduation."

"Another nutty organization begun by Beverly Kimes; it was a rainy day, and it seemed like the thing to do. I started a Virgin Chapter. We hereby swear, that I won't! The following signed up: Bev Kimes (Pres); Beverly Schuer, (V. Pres); Laurie Vesely (Exec Sec.); Pamela Horsely (Treasurer); Diane Dowdall (Virgin Historian); and Ann Sergel (Virgin Disciplinarian)."

"Constitution. *** Be it enacted *** that Alpha Chapter of the Vestal Virgin Society, is hereby instituted on this twelfth day of February, nineteen hundred sixty-one and, for the purpose of perpetuating virginity among unmarried women."

There were rules and standards set forth for this organization, (I won't go into all that), but, I will tell you a couple of things: Their motto: Have virginity —

28

won't travel. *Help!* (by the Beatles), was their vestal virgin song.

"Here's to our virginity. Here's to our chastity, too. Here's to the vows we've pledged to keep; which keeps us from what we might like to do. Here's to the girls within the group; few and far between. Vestal Virgins all — heed our call. Help; Come running here before you fall."

"After the Big V, became old hat, Sharon T. and I launched a "Try To get Some Culture and Knowledge" club. Most were enthused, but one called us 'culture vultures.' Notes for a discussion group asked: "Would you like to prove Homer's theory wrong? 'In youth and beauty, wisdom is but rare — Homer.' The discussion will be of Theta U. Forum. Anyone interested, contact Bev Kimes or Sharon Thompson."

"I was about to be a Theatre Alum — almost killed me to fill out the card." "After June, what? I began looking into graduate school possibility. I decided on Penn State: the entire story is told in the correspondence below."

Between February 2, 1961 thru June 13, 1961 her scrapbook contained 13 pieces of correspondence regarding Penn State.

May 18, 1961, a letter from Walter H. Walters, Department Head of Theatre Arts, offered: "Three options: one quarter-time assistantship in Journalism at $756.00, plus exemption from fees; one quarter-time assistantship in Theatre Arts at $756.00 plus exemption from fees — you would assist me in Theatre Management; and lastly, one half-time assistant, split between Journalism and Theatre Arts at $1512.00, plus exemption from fees. I hope we haven't made things complicated for you. We feel that you can handle the split responsibilities, if you wished, or could choose between the first two. Any one of the three, will be quite satisfactory with this department and journalism." Beverly opted for Option three.

On February 17,1961, Bev was appointed to the President's Panel and worked with President Henry and other activity leaders. As campus leader, she wrote: "I was a member of Mortar Board Selection, and of Torch Council. The Torch Council will be considering the eligibility of the present sophomore women for membership in Torch next year."

On March 16, 1961, an invitation from the Illini Union and the Alumni Association read: "We invite you to attend the annual 100 Banquet, in honor of the one-hundred outstanding senior activity leaders".

A letter dated April 13, 1961, from Theodore Peterson, Dean, read:
"Dear Beverly, Irene Pierson, of the Illini Union, has   just told me that you are among the 96 outstanding seniors chosen to be honored at the 100 Banquet. On behalf of the faculty, I would like to congratulate you on being selected for this recognition of your achievement. Your selection is an honor to the College as well as to you, and we all are very proud of you." Bev said of the banquet, "A delightful dinner and a rewarding experience."

Pi of Theta Sigma Phi, sponsored the 34th Annual Matrix Table and Guest Speaker, Dorothy Powers (the first woman journalist to receive The Ernie Pyle Memorial Award). "Two awards will be presented at the Banquet: Outstanding Senior Women in College of Journalism and Communication, and the Shirley Kreasen Strout Award, a scholarship set up in Mrs. Strout's honor by Zeta Tau Alpha Foundation, in recognition of her many years of active service. Miss Marjorie Tepper, of Chicago, Matrix Table Chairman, and Miss Beverly Kimes, Publicity Chairman will oversee the reservations."

Beverly corresponded with the guest speaker. After the banquet, Bev wrote in her scrapbook, "I was even luckier and terribly thrilled to be voted the Outstanding Woman in Journalism. Being presented at the Banquet was wonderful." A hand written note from Judy Bednar, her pledge daughter, said: "Congratulations, to The Bestest 'Mommy' in The World.

A news article in the Chicago Tribune read:
Wheaton Senior Gets Journalism Honors. Miss Beverly Kimes, of 515 S. Hale Street, Wheaton, recently was named outstanding 1961 graduate of the University of Illinois, College of Journalism and Communications. She also received the Outstanding Graduate Award from Pi chapter of Theta Sigma Phi, national journalism fraternity. Miss Kimes plans to do graduate work in journalism at Pennsylvania State University.

At the Curtain Call Banquet on Tuesday, May 28, 1961, ten people received University of Illinois Theatre Honor achievement awards. Beverly was one of them. Her note read: "My exit as General Manager, the Curtain Call Banquet. My nameplate and picture came down."

Bev served, again, as a Rush Counselor for June of 1961. "It was a riot at LAR, with about 500 rushes and fourteen other Counselors." She graduated on, June 17, 1961, with a Bachelor of Science Degree in Com- munications. There, to celebrate the occasion with her, were Mom, Dad, sis- ter, Sharon and Aunt Olive.

Beverly at graduation time

A letter written on August 24, 1961, from Joseph W. Scott, Executive Director of The University Theatre, read: "Dear Bev: The time is growing close for you to take off on your new venture at Penn State. I

31

wish you all the success in the world; and remember all my little sermons on maintaining your ego and self confidence. You well know that I have the greatest respect for your abilities, and know that you will succeed in whatever you undertake. I am most grateful to you Bev, for all the work and devotion which you have given to this organization. It meant a great deal while you were here; and in many ways, your influence will continue, even though you are not here."

The following is Beverly's notes about leaving the University:

"I left the University of Illinois, the University Theatre, and my friends — though it was a tearful farewell. I have the happy memory of the four most happy years of my life, thus far. I shall never forget it. I was a lucky girl. I left the university in good standing and with considerable success behind me. I left the university with many more friends, such as Judy Bednar, my pledge daughter, who sent me a kind and touching graduation card."

The card from Judy read: "Dear Bev, There are no words that can express my admiration and respect for you. Aside from being a true intellectual, you also have a deep understanding of 'all' types of people; and this, above all, has left a lasting impression on me. I'll never forget you, Bev, nor what you stand for — a near perfect being! Good Luck always 'Mom.' Love, Judy."

"To the University of Illinois, I owe a great deal; I only hope I will always be worthy of the fine education I received there. Next year, Pennsylvania State, and Graduate School!"

If you recall, I mentioned Bev's statement that she made at the close of high school: "Despite the honors received, I never looked on my high school years as successful. I never hit the top; I was secretary, treasurer, had a small part, was a member, but, I never lead or had the lead. I look forward to college for these goals." Beverly achieved these goals... in spades.

Chapter 3:
Years at Penn State

Bev returned home for her last summer job at Sears, and to leave her college scrapbooks in the care of her mother. These, along with all the childhood memories, would stay in the care of Grace until the mid- eighties.

On one of our trips to visit her folks years later, her Mom said, "Beverly, I have been the caretaker much too long and it's time for you to take the boxes from under the bed and take them with you." It's a good thing that, at the time, we had a large building!

Beverly entered Penn State, around the beginning of September of 1961. For her Masters, she chose Journalism as a major and Theater Arts as her Minor. That Fall, Bev made a couple of trips into New York City to visit the New York City Library, the Met and off-Broadway for a few shows. Perhaps, she was also feeling out the new place she would later call home.

She had a graduate assistantship as Assistant to the Producer, Mr. Walters, from September 1961 to June 1962. She also did research for the School of Journalism from September 1961 to June 1962.

In 1962, she became Director of the Department of Theater Arts. As Director, her job from June 1962 to September 1963 included Publicity and Public Relations. She also worked with the Mateer Playhouse, (a Professional Resident Company) in Neff Mills, Pennsylvania, and managed Publicity and Public Relations for the Pavilion Theater, (a Professional Resident Company), University Park, at State College.

As Director, she had the responsibility of writing reviews for the plays and placing advertisements for plays

34

coming up. To place the ads, posters and reviews, she would travel weekly around the area to such towns as Altoona, Huntington, Lewistown, Lock Haven and Phillipsburg. She placed her posters at her regular weekly stops, as well as at other random locations. This was quite a day trip. Some of her other duties included organizing dinner-theater packages, parties, and setting up regional ticket sales outlets. Years later, when Bev and I would be driving west on Route 80 and pass by the area, she liked to reminisce about these travels. They held very fond memories for her.

Bev made specific mention in her scrap books of two ladies at newspapers where she visited: Jo McMeen, a friend at *The Huntington Daily News*, and Pat Hinton of *The Altoona Mirror*. Added to one of Bev's press releases to announce a play being held over, Pat added a note: "Beverly Kimes, the lovely promotions and public relations gal, with whom we have had some excellent public relations. It would be nice to have Bev follow through with journalism for newspaper. She has a fine style."

For the Mateer and Pavilion Theater, Beverly developed extensive reports for all the plays. These reports included detailed attendance by day, a recap of the total attending each play, as well as a percentage of total attendance compared to the capacity that could be seated in both theaters. She also reported on how many people attended each performance from surrounding towns, separated by each town, and how many theater dinner packages and theater parties were sold for each play.

A note in the college news WDFM Schedule, about what's going on mentioned: "This Wednesday June 28, Pavilion Theater preview — Max Fischer, Director of The Waltz of the Toreadors, discusses the play with Beverly Kimes."

"Beverly's Lament "
Work several weeks to get a poster into a store,
Pass by the next morning and it isn't there anymore.
Get an important interview with a star at eight,
Happily he turns up only two hours late.
Morning paper ran last week's ad,
And you ask me why I look so sad?

Write in all our papers about our air cooled ease,
Next morning the system breaks down and its
ninety degrees.
Work hard to get an advertiser to visit our show,
No one around to talk to him who's in the know.
Everyone wants bigger print for their name,
Sparkle you say, though I don't feel the same.
You read the books on how to do it,
They give you all kinds of advice.
Maybe, if the authors went out to do it,
They'd turn around and think twice
About writing.

The one important day that I have to go very far,
That's the only day I can't get the company car.
Posters have to be distributed around the town by eight,
When they were delivered, saw they had the wrong date.
Guess I'll keep on smiling just as much as I can,
It's all in the life of a publicity woman.

The following was included in a proposal dated May, 31, 1961, from *McCall's Magazine* to the School of Journalism, Pennsylvania State University:

"There is an editorial project getting under way here at McCall's which has to do jointly with magazines and colleges. I am wondering whether you would be kind enough to give me the benefit of your opinion and suggestions about it, both on its merits and on the manner in which you think your college could participate."

"What we have in mind is to designate — and pay — a number of college groups, (probably classes in journalism) to make a continuing study of McCall's as a

36

class project and to report their finding to us along lines set out in the enclosed information sheet. Generally, we would be looking for helpful criticism. The basic purpose as far as we are concerned would be to provide grass-roots information for the editors, although certainly it could be a constructive experience for the students as well. Whether such analysis could be integrated generally into the work of an individual class, I don't know, although the journalism people that we have talked with think it can be. We are prepared to pay the sum of $250.00 per month to the class or group, for whatever use it cares to make, for the nine months of the college year starting in September. There also will be a $500.00 bonus in June to the group which has produced the best single report."

After a few more pieces of correspondence, The Pennsylvania University and McCall's agreed to the following: The Magazine Journalism class would do the reports. The $250.00 per report would be paid to the university, and the $500.00 bonus would be paid to the group that produced the best single report.

Beverly and three other graduate students were assigned this project, the four held discussions as a group, and Beverly would type up their opinions and findings. There were eight reports done between October 1961 and May 1962. On October 9,1961, Eugene Goodwin, Director of the School of Journalism wrote to Beverly: "I was very pleased with your first report for *McCalls,* and I'm sure they will be also. You may have a very good chance of winning the $500.00 bonus." (I have no knowledge of what the outcome of this was.)

Research done for the School of Journalism from 1961-1962, included a paper which Bev wrote on UNESCO and International Journalism Education, dated May 28,1962. This paper focused on the UNESCO efforts in the field of international journalism education, since the UNESCO-sponsored International Expert Meeting on Professional Training for Journalists, held in April of 1956.

Research material was found predominantly in

37

UNESCO periodicals and documents, although American and British newspaper indices and trade journals in the field were also consulted. The paper was divided into three chapters: Chapter One traces the UNESCO project since the Paris meeting; Chapter Two presented an idealistic overview of the project, and Chapter Three was a critical, closer view. To give some prospective to the UNESCO project, a summary of existing education facilities for journalists in the various countries of the world, is presented in the appendix. The report was 45 pages. The comment of the Professor on the front cover: "Very good, no further comment, J.B.M."

In addition to journalism and theater, Beverly also studied History and English. Her Master Thesis was on H.L. Mencken. It was an 8-½" by11" 200-page hardbound book. For those not familiar with Mencken, a brief biography follows:

H. L. Mencken, September 12th 1880–January 29th 1956
NEWSPAPERMAN -CRITIC, ESSAYIST-PHILOLOGIST

"I was a larva of the comfortable and complacent bourgeoisie... encapsulated in affection, and kept fat, and saucy and contented. Thus I got though my nonage without acquiring an inferiority complex...," so Mencken introduces a long, loud and loquacious life.

He was born into a cigar-making family. Mencken had no interest in the business of his grandfather and father, however he was forced to work in it until his father died in January 13, 1889. It was beautiful letters, not pungent cigars that marked and made his life.

Christmas 1888, he was given a boy's press that gave him his first smell of printer's ink. It was this gift that gave birth to the famous signature, H. L. Mencken. (In the process of learning to use the set, all of the lower case "r" letters were smashed, and Mencken was forced to reduce his first name from Henry to "H." Other presents came and went, but he claimed that there was never another that fetched and floored him like Dorman's Baltimore No 10

38

Self–Inker Printing Press.

As a boy, Mencken attended F. Knapp's Institute, and later the, Polytechnic. Mencken's own account of his life up to his twelfth year, in *Happy Days* is a delightful account of bourgeoisie boyhood and Baltimore in the eighties. In his next experience with print, *Huckleberry Finn*, he referred to it as, "...probably the most stupendous event of my whole life. Thus launched upon the career of a bookworm, I presently began to reach out right and left for more fodder."

On January 13, 1889, the Monday following the death of his father he presented himself in the city room of the old *Baltimore Morning Herald*. After turning up every night for a month, he was sent off to cover news in a rural suburb. From that night, Mencken was a newspaperman. He advanced at an alarming rate, to city editor and, two years later, Managing Editor of the Herald. In 1906, when the Herald closed, Mencken went to the Sunpapers as Sunday Editor. In 1911, he started his column, "the Free Lance" in the Evening Sun. He began another series of weekly articles in 1919, and was associated with the Sunpapers, except for one short break, until 1948.

Mencken immortalized and deflated the twenties. Only one who was young, adult and literate during Mencken's hay-day, could realize the impact he had on his times. He was a critic of ideals in a smug world with the "old time journalist's concept of himself as a free lance spirit and darling of the gods, licensed by his high merits to ride and deride the visible universe." An iconoclast with an invective style, he became the terror, first of Baltimore, then of the Republic. (For more on Mencken visit the Enoch Pratt Free Library, Baltimore Maryland.)

Mencken was Beverly's hero. It was said by many, that if Bev exercised her Mencken on you, in letter or note form, you may need to consult a dictionary to understand the written word.

The following are letters to acknowledge some of

Bev's achievements during that time:

A letter, dated November 1, 1962, from John M. Harrison, Faculty Adviser, read: "Dear Beverly, It is a pleasure to inform you that Kappa Tau Alpha, honorary scholarship society in journalism and communications, has selected you for membership. The Penn State Chapter of Kappa Tau Alpha was established in 1956, one of more than 40 chapters over the country. One of the society's chief purposes is to recognize and award outstanding scholarship in our field. Your election to membership is based on your grade point average and on character recommendations of the Journalism School faculty. Membership in Kappa Tau Alpha, which is for life, is extended to undergraduates and graduate honor students, together with faculty members. As advisor to the Penn State Chapter, let me congratulate you on your achievements which have earned you this recognition. Sincerely John M. Harrison"

A letter from H.K. Schilling, Dean date May 16, 1963 stated: "Dear Miss Kimes, It is a pleasure to inform you of your selection as Graduate Student Marshal for commencement on June 9, 1963. This is a significant honor

of which you may be justly proud. Your duties, which are very modest, will be outlined for you by the University Marshal, Professor David H. McKinley. Congratulations on your past achievements and best wishes for the future. Sincerely Yours, H. K. Schilling, Dean".

Beverly, Student Marshal for the Graduate School at June commencement, Penn State University

At note dated May 26, 1963from the Penn State Players stated: "This is to certify that, Beverly Kimes, has been approved and initiated and is, hereby, declared to be a full member of The Penn State Players."

Beverly Graduated on June 12, 1963 and received her Master of Arts with a Major in Journalism. In

40

attendance, were her Mother, her sister Sharon and Aunt Olive.

Bev started to look for employment after graduation. She applied to five companies between May and August of 1963, with no luck or possibilities. It was time to leave State College and head East to what has been her desired destination for years... The Big Apple, New York City.

During that time, Bev received a letter from Elliott Hardaway, Director of Libraries, dated September 4,1963. It read: "Dear Miss Kimes, Mr Wolff, a new member of the University of South Florida faculty, has brought us a copy of Burris-Meyer's Theaters and Auditoriums which you and Miss Clay so generously presented to this library on the occasion of Mr. Wolff's joining this faculty. We are very pleased to have this volume, the definite work in its area , added to our library. We know that it will be useful to both our faculty and students."

"Should you visit Florida anytime, we would like to invite you to come to Tampa and visit our University. We believe you would be interested in seeing what has been accomplished in all areas, but especially in your field of the theater. We would also like to show you the library and tell you something of what we are trying to accomplish, Sincerely Yours, Elliott Hardaway."

After graduation, Bev remained in touch with her classmates, William and Rosemary Jackson. Both Bill and Rosemary had returned to Penn State for graduate school, majoring in journalism. Friends for life, Bill always liked to say that he knew Bev long before she knew anything about automobiles.

In a letter to me explaining how they had met, Bill wrote: "Among the other journalism grad students was a tall, attractive young lady from Illinois named Beverly Rae Kimes, who was minoring in Theater Arts. Rosemary, who had been active in the Penn State Theater Group as an undergraduate, took a couple theater arts classes with

41

Beverly, and we three became friends though our mutual interests."

At the time they met, Bill was very involved in automobiles. He raced sports cars in the Sports Car Club of America national races and hill climbs in 1956 and 1957. While serving in the Army in Germany, he raced with the Hesse Motor Sports Club in the LeMans Retrospective in 1958 in a 1935 BMW 315/1 roadster.

Over the next two years, Bill hosted parties for journalism grad students. From time to time, Bill invited some of his racing car buddies, who would arrive in their MG's, Jaguars and Triumphs. "Bev was very taken by my last race car, which I was still using as an everyday driver a 1957 AC Bristol Roadster," Bill admitted.

Bill became the Editor of *Antique Automobile* in 1962. He was also past editor of *Classic Car, Blub Horn,* and a co-author with Gorden Buehrig on *Rolling Sculpture.* Bill was also a contributing writer for other car publications and a Founding Member of The Society of Automotive Historians, founded in October of 1969. (The meeting to form the society was held in Bill's office at Antique Automobile in Hershey Pa.)

On June 1, 1970, Bill and Rosemary purchased *The Sun Newspaper* which served the Hershey and Hummelstown areas. Their time, from June of 1970 until November 2007, was mostly spent running the newspaper.

When visiting New York for the New York Auto Shows, Bill and Rosemary would stay with Bev and me. We would eat dinner at Dresner's Restaurant (a favorite of theirs from their past, during their early years of courtship.) Bill and Rosemary hosted Bev and me in their home over the past ten years during the Annual Hershey Fall Meet.

According to Bill, "Bev and I both at least partially attributed our success in doing automotive research for an excellent class taught Dr. Fred Marbut, a former Washington Post Staffer. He really drilled us on how to find information using all sorts of libraries from those locally, to the Library of Congress."

Chapter 4:
The Move To New York

I am not quite sure, just exactly when Beverly arrived in New York. I believe, that it would have been around the first part of July of1963. She, and a girlfriend, were moved there by a fellow student with his old Volkswagon bus. Bev recalled "It was a very long, hot trip. There wasn't any air conditioning; It was a hot July day, and the old V.W. didn't go very fast."

For a short time, the girls shared an old walk-up apartment on the Upper West Side. Bev told me that she often met some pretty shady characters in the stairway when she was coming or going. One day, she had just gotten back to her apartment from an interview, and secured the multiple locks. (In New York, having more than one lock is not uncommon.)

All of a sudden, there was a very loud banging on the door, and a very loud voice said: "This is the police, open the door." It took her a couple of minutes, due to a high level of anxiety and multiple locks, to get the door opened. The policeman responded, "What did you do, flush the stuff down the toilet?" Between sob's and tears, she said she don't know what he was talking about. It seems that this building had a lot of drug deals going down. The policeman, who soon came to the conclusion that she was not involved with the drug deals in any way, departed.

Beverly and her girlfriend began to look for other places to live right away. I am not sure where her girlfriend went. In haste to move, Beverly took refuge, for a few weeks, with a cousin and her husband, Bob and Kim O'Rourk, who lived in University Heights.

Beverly moved to 215 East 80th Street in August

of 1963. The area was suggested by Bill Jackson's wife, Rosemary, who had lived in New York in the 1960's. Bev's mother was so happy to hear that she now lived in a place with a 24-hour-a-day doorman. Her first apartment, LD, she shared with another friend, Nedra Clay. Neither woman had a job at the time. Times were lean, and often dinner was ground chuck.

Nedra wanted to become an actor, and Bev was still trying to find a position with some sort of theatrical connection. The apartment was a small studio. There was not much room, but they managed. Bev told me that she and Nedra would sometimes go out on the streets at night and gather boards and blocks that had been left at the curb for the garbage men to take away. They used them to make book shelves and a couple of small tables.

In March of 1965, the friends parted ways. Bev had a job; Nedra was still trying. Bev moved up a few floors to a one bedroom apartment 8G, and Nedra moved to Jackson Heights, Queens. Around the end of 1966 or beginning of 1967, Bev moved back downstairs to apartment, LB. She had gotten word from the door man (In New York, the doorman knows everything!), that the young lady in LB was going to move. Bev spoke to the building Super, John Martone, to see if she could have the apartment, and he said, yes. Bev went and introduced herself to the departing tenant, and even helped her pack.

This was a downward move for Bev because this apartment was right off the lobby; but it was a big step up in living quarters. LB was a two-bedroom, two-bathroom apartment with a very large living room, small kitchen and dining area. It also faced 80th Street, which was a plus.

Beverly and me on the street by the terrace by our apartment, circa 1982

When I first met Bev, she had told me, "One thing you must understand. This is where I live, and I don't intend to move; so don't bring

45

up the subject." At that time, I was living and working in Northern New Jersey. I became a commuter, and did so for the next 27 years. She lived in that apartment until her passing in May of 2008; a total of 45 years.

Around the late 60's, Bev's mom, Grace, re-entered the work force. She purchased a new Yellow Ford Mustang, and had a gotten a position with Avon Cosmetics as a sales person. Grace was quite proud of her first car, as was Beverly. She even sent her mom a Mustang poster that had been done by *Automobile Quarterly*. Anna, Bev's grandmother, liked the Mustang, as well. Grace would pick her up from the Nursing home once a week, and take her for long drives in the country.

After about a year, Grace had established quite a customer base. She became the top sales person for her region, and made the President's list, time after time. Once, Grace was called in by the I.R.S. for a tax audit. When she arrived for the interview, she had a box of receipts with her. These receipts were written on everything from bits of paper to Popsicle sticks. Not too long into the interview, the I.R.S. agent became so frustrated, that he just accepted her tax return and ended the inquiry.

Beverly was very proud of her mother's achievements, and absolutely loved the story of Grace's encounter with the Internal Revenue Service. I am not quite sure how long Grace worked with Avon, but my best guess would be, until the mid seventies. Like mother, like daughter, she did her best, kept good records and didn't throw anything out.

Through the efforts of Lillian Roberts Personnel, Bev got her first job. The agency's fee was $214.00. When she went to her interview with Scott Baily at *Automobile Quarterly*, she told him, "The only thing I know about automobiles, is that I have a driver's license." That didn't deter Mr. Baily. He had sufficient background information from her resume and reference letters to know that she could fill the job.

46

She was hired as an editorial assistant in September of 1963, at a salary of $90.00 a week. Bev once told me, " I could have made more as a secretary." (But, of course, she had no interest in being a secretary.) "I took the job, simply as a means to pay the bills, and it would look good on my resume ,when I found a job that I liked and wanted." Fate, however, sent her from what she considered a temporary job, down the road to a lifetime career.

I firmly believe, that one of the reasons Bev stayed at *Automobile Quarterly*, was due to Henry Austin Clark, Jr.,

of Glen Cove, New York. At the time, he was a contributing writer and consultant to A. Q. He preferred to be addressed as Austie. (He often said: "Mr. Clark is my father.") He was a long-time old car buff and collector; starting around 1936, while he was still in college. He was also the owner of the Long Island Automobile Museum in South Hampton N.Y. Austie is a legend in old car hobby circles. He took Beverly for her first ride in an antique car, a 1903 Curved Dash Oldsmobile.

Austie at his desk in Glen Cove, NY, 1980

They traveled from the Mercer garage in the Bronx, to the New York World's Fair, in Flushing Meadow, on June 26, 1964. The event — the Oldsmobile Curved Dash Rally — was sponsored by Oldsmobile. The Clark's, Austie and his wife, Wallita, would remain our lifelong friends

Automobile Quarterly was in its second year of publication at the time, and the offices were located at 515 Madison Ave. Beverly moved up through the ranks at a good pace: Assistant Editor in January,1964; Associate Editor in1965; Managing Editor in1967; and Editor-in-Chief from1975 to 1981. When she left the publication, the circulation had doubled. At the time, subscriptions were about 32,000, and the renewal rate was 90 percent. It's my firm opinion (as well as that of others including publisher, Scott Baily), that A. Q. would not have become what it was without her.

47

Her writing style was among the best of authors of the time. And, over the years, she would grow to be the most recognized automobile writer and historian in the country. In September, 1983, *Life Magazine* referred to her

as the nation's top automobile scholar. Her friendly and helpful attitude was ever present. Her dedication to research and details, as well as her dedication to the job, were outstanding. Her mentor was Ken Purdy, writer and author of *Kings of the Road*. Over the years, Bev would become the mentor to many struggling authors, as well.

Beverly's work space at A.Q., 515 Madison Ave., NY

The following are quotes and notes from what others have said or written to Bev during this time:

Chip Miller, York, Pa. Author of *The Corvette Restoration Guide*. "It's been a pleasure working on this project with you. I'm not sure why, but I expected Beverly Rae Kimes to be a lady twice your age. Guess I figured anyone who writes that good, had to be around for awhile. At any rate, I was pleasantly surprised. You are a young lady with a lot of talent and drive. Just think of how many masterpieces you will have written, when you are twice your age."

Terry Dunham, Apopka, Fl., wrote: "You simply have no idea how much I appreciated your help and guidance over the last five years. Simply put, there would have been no *Buick Book* without you, and for me, it was a dream come true."

Gorden Buehrig , Legendary Automotive Designer "Beverly I don't believe I have ever told you, how pleased I am with your success at *Automobile Quarterly*. You, not only are one of the best writers in the business, you are also one of the best

Gorden Buehrig with Bev, early 80's

48

in doing your research. Obviously, you must be a great executive to be the Editor."

Charles M. Jorden, Director of Design, General Motors, wrote: "It was certainly a pleasure to have you visit the General Motors design staff. You are the most enthusiastic historian that I ever met."

Russ Catlin, Cuyahoga Falls, Ohio — Editor/writer, wrote: "I also wrote Scott that during my 75 years, I have worked with, and for, a great many editors. Some bad, some good, but you stood head and shoulders above all in the talent, productivity and inspiration, and I mean that in the fullest professional sense. I know your style and format so well you could ghost write a new Lord's Prayer and I'd know who wrote it."

Michael Lamm, Stockton California — Lamm-Morodo Publishing, wrote: "Part of my reason for this note, is to tell you that you're in the tradition of Edward Bok. You encourage and bring along your writers. You don't know how much that is appreciated."

Anthony Young, Ridgefield, Connecticut — Freelance writer, wrote: "My working relationship with you was ideal; no... it was idyllic. You were always receptive to my suggestions; your responses were faster than a speeding bullet, and even your cheery rejections made me feel good. After awhile, I realized you are one of a kind (I won't say were!), in magazine publishing. All editors should be modeled after you. There would be fewer freelance casualties."

Walt Gosden, Floral Park, New York — Historian/writer, wrote: "I am truly personally very glad that you enjoyed working on the story. Your kind words, alone, made all those years of frustration of not being able to find out much about De Causse, all worthwhile."

I mentioned early on in this book about Bev's name. Since Beverly could be of male gender in Europe, and Rae was her middle name, it was thought that "she" must be "he." She was often addressed in correspondences as Mr. Kimes. On one occasion, a letter from Mr. Charles A. Kirby of Portsmouth, Ohio questioned, "*Automobile Quarterly*. It would be interesting to know if Beverly Rae Kimes is a Mr. or Mrs. He, or she, writes great. The article about 1927 was a masterpiece. A.Q. is the first thing I look for, when I can relax and have the time to read through it."

Bev told me, once, that the editor of the English magazine, *Autocar*, paid a visit to A.Q. She corresponded with him for a few years. When he was greeted by Beverly, he said "I would like to see Beverly Rae Kimes." To this, Bev replied, "Well, you are looking at her." Needless to say, he was a little astounded. By the time it was known that she was, indeed a "she," it didn't really matter.

In April of 1966, Beverly was invited on a press junket from Italy to New York, by Alfa-Romeo of Milan. A letter from Giuseppe Luraghi, President of Alfa, wrote: "It is with great pleasure that we have learned you will able to pay us a visit early next month. I look forward to meeting you personally, and assure you that Alfa-Romeo will do its upmost to insure a comfortable and informative trip." She was doing a story on the New Alfa-Romeo 1600.

Bev was the youngest journalist, and the only female journalist on the trip, so she was given the royal treatment. As the only lady among all those gentlemen, on one occasion after setting sail, she was asked if perhaps, she would like to start by giving the group something of the historic background of the Spider 1600. She did, starting with the earliest history of the company, up to the Spider1600. Of the 1600, she said: "All Alfa Romeos look like winners, even standing still. The new 1600, with its cleanness and continuity of line, looks fast. And, that is in the Alfa Romeo tradition."

The ship, Raffaello, set sail on May 11 for its voyage to New York. For the entire voyage, Bev sat at the president's table between Giuseppe Luragi and Count Giovanni Lurani, whom she met going through customs. They became fast friends, since the Count had been a race car driver. The Raffaello Dinner Menu on Tuesday May 17 was dedicated, "In Honor of Beverly R. Kimes."

After dinner every night, the three would take walks together on the decks. There was a little infatuation between the Count and Beverly; I'm sure, but strictly platonic. However, before the Count departed to go back home, he presented Beverly with a lovely diamond and emerald broach.

In 1970, *Automobile Quarterly* moved its offices to 221 Nassau Street in Princeton, New Jersey. Beverly didn't want to move to Princeton, so, she took an apartment there that A. Q. rented for her. She commuted between New York and Princeton for the next 10 years.

Bev at her desk at A.Q.

Bev's responsibilities grew as the magazine did. The wide range of experience included; "... organizing a research library, historical archives and reference card catalog, setting up photographic files, devising editorial and production procedures, collaborating on promotion pieces. Editorial work has included: story planning, extensive research, writing, acquisition, re-writing, copyediting, captions, titles. Coordinating a multi-national network of photographers has been in my charge. Staffs under my direction have varied in numbers from two to a dozen or more in-house editors and editorial assistants, research associates and contributing editors both in the United States and abroad. Considerable travel has been the norm."

Beverly did not like doing captions. In a memo to Stan Grayson, at A.Q., she stated, "I hate doing captions. Please look these over and tell me they're terrific." His reply: "I have looked these over and they are terrific." For the inscription in Stan Grayson's copy of the *Classic Era*,

Beverly in the rumble seat of a Rover automobile, 1967

she wrote in her lovely hand: "Ask me a question, and I'll give you a pageant."

In addition to being Editor and Chief of *Automobile Quarterly*, in1971, she also became the Editorial Director

Beverly in Hershey at A.Q.'s tent, 1980

of Princeton Publishing Company, a book division of *Automobile Quarterly*. With the launch of its Library Series Book Division, Automobile Quarterly Publications grew to be the world's largest publisher of automobile history. Between 1971 and 1981, the book division published 19 books. They ranged from anthologies to a ghostwritten corporate history; to a how-to restoration guide; as well as full-scale histories of American Motor Cars.

In Bev's notes, two specific references were made to *The Packard Book*, an 828-page history of the car and the company. She coordinated the efforts of 16 Packard historians, rewrote or edited the text, organized picture research, provided all supplementary material and supervised production. This project was so lengthy and intense, that at the conclusion, she had strained her eyes so badly, that she had to start wearing eye glasses. The other book, *The Cars That Henry Ford Built,* which she authored, was the only book taken on the first trade-exchange mission with China.

During her 18 years with A.Q., Bev had 58 magazine credits, 21 of which used pseudonyms or were unsigned. The reason for this, was that only one article by a single author could appear in a single issue. Beverly always had articles written ahead to fill in gaps when needed. When this occurred, she would assign fictitious names to these articles. One such name, was Cullen Thomas (the name of her nephew) Bev told me Cullen even got fan mail!

Bev authored three books: *The Cars that Henry Ford Built, the Golden Anniversary of the Lincoln Motor Car,* and *Oldsmobile: The First Seventy Years.* She co-authored *A*

History of the Motor Car and the Company; Great Cars and Grand Marques with Richard Langworth, Editor of *Packard;* as well as a book on overall automobile hobby collecting. Beverly was Editorial Director for 14 books, and ghostwriter for ten others.

During her years with A.Q., she was not permitted to belong to individual clubs, or to receive awards for her work under her own name. Thus, early awards from The Society of Automotive Historians went to *Automobile Quarterly*, including the 1978 Cugnot Award for *The Nash Story*; 1979 Cugnot Award for *The Packard : A History of the Motor Car and the Company.* She received two Gold Awards from NEOGRAPHICS, for books (hardbound) / 3 or more colors, for *The Packard Book* and Magazines, *Automobile Quarterly* Vol. 16.

Her major research sources included her favorite: the Detroit Public Library — the Automotive History Collection. Over the years, she would travel there many times, and would spend several days in the dusty stacks. Each morning, she would arrive with her sack of dimes, so she could feed the copy machine. Due to this habit, she was nicknamed the Dime Lady.

Other research sources included the collection of Ralph Dunnwoodie, a former curator for the Harrah Automobile Collection in Reno, Nevada; the automotive library of Henry Austin Clark, in Glen Cove New York; and last, but not least, the New York Main Library on 5th Ave at 42nd Street, as well as several other of its branches.

In 2008, The Automotive History Collection commissioned Ken Dalhousie, a famous Automobile Artist, to paint a portrait of Beverly. This was unveiled at a special gathering in January 2009, and now hangs in the most appropriate place, above the copy machine in the main reading room of the Detroit library.

The real success of Beverly's writing came from her relentless research, dedication to facts, hard work, and style of writing. She researched the entire history of the automobile, including not only the automobiles themselves, but the men and the companies that were the innovators, and the factories that produced them. I know that she loved the movers and makers as much, if not more, than the automobiles themselves. Let us not forget the scoundrels (as there were many, as in any new venture); and she sorted those out very well.

In her book, *Pioneers, Engineers and Scoundrels*, published in 2005, she told the whole story about the subject so beautifully. Of this book she said, "I have been writing this book in bits and pieces for over 40 years, and it is my most favorite work to date."

Here are some quotes from people who wrote to her about the book:

Kim Strickler, typesetter, wrote: "What a pleasant surprise to receive a signed copy of your latest book *"Pioneers, Engineers and Scoundrels."* This was such a great story to typeset. I was intrigued at chapter one, as I keyed in the copy! You're such a terrific writer! Eric and I were both humbled and flattered with your kind words to us in the Acknowledgments section of the book. We look forward to 'reading' this book again! You are such a thoughtful and generous person; and we treasure your friendship in our lives. Thank you again for sending it to us."

The New York Times

Pioneers, Engineers, and Scoundrels
The Dawn of the Automobile in America
By Beverly Rae Kimes
Illustrated. 558 pages. SAE International. $39.95.

Beverly Rae Kimes has written an absolutely delightful book, both entertaining and informative, on one of the world's great inventions, the automobile. It is a chronological study of the cars as well as the inventors, engineers, businessmen and con artists who made horseless carriage history from the 1800's through the 1920's.

Ms. Kimes presents the very human side of the development of this dynamic industry. All

Michael Kellerm wrote: "Marvelous, simply marvelous; surely my humble words will not properly or adequately praise your most recent volume of automotive history. Stated most simply, Bev, your account of the early years of the motorcar industry is a classic, a masterpiece."

By 1981, the relationship between Beverly and Baily at A.Q. had deteriorated, and had been for some time; and

Bev riding Abduhl, the camel, during a trip to Egypt

Somewhere in Europe; Bev enjoying the ride

Monticello Raceway, circa 1970, Time out for a little fun; Bev bet on horses whose names she liked.

Beverly said she could no longer tolerate the situation. For Bev, It had become unbearable, and it was time to leave.

Beverly submitted her letter of resignation on January 5, 1981. She gave two months notice, so that the magazine might take a smooth transition to a new editor. Baily accepted her resignation and in a letter which he wrote the following day, said: "No one person could possibly replace you. Perhaps this in itself is a telling testament that reveals the great pressure of responsibility you have assumed as our company grew and our editorial staff shrank. Your burden has been tremendous and carried on under the most difficult circumstances to faultless perfection with devotion and a professional sense of loyalty to all. Your high standards have marked us well."

The following are notes to Bev upon her departure from A.Q.: C. L. Haines Jr., Lauredale, Pennsylvania — Historian /Freelance writer wrote: "I want you to know that I'm sorry that you are leaving Automobile Quarterly Publications and, if that includes *Automobile Quarterly* magazine, I'm especially sorry. As a charter subscriber, I'm well aware of the impact you've had on its success."

Keith Marvin, — Historian /Freelance writer, wrote: "Keep me abreast of your plans, as they work out. I fervently hope you will remain in the writing world. Your stories have such an original touch to them. It would be hard, indeed, to even visualize an automotive world without them."

Norm Hilton, Chicago, Illnois — Subscriber wrote: "Thanks for giving me back my childhood. I wish there were words that I could use, to say how much your magazine means to me. Each story, for me, brings back some remembrance of the past; with a sense of how valuable and important people are, whether they succeed or fail. To me, your stories convey a gracious sense of personal

worth and dignity that, in the long run, will leave a stronger impression than even the fine photographs."

Miles Coverdale, Beverly and Jeff Scott, Manhattan, circa 1970.

John Peckham — Historian/Artist, wrote: "I'm sure you realize that you have quite a few friends in "Automobile Land" and we all wish you the very, very best. We all feel that you are one of the really special people."

Automobile Quarterly, until it was sold to CBS Publications; and Bev did not write for the magazine during that time. CBS didn't keep the publication very long, and Kutztown Publishing Company, (which had printed A.Q. for a long time), bought it to protect their printing rights. They later sold it to Gerry Durnell, and it moved to Albany, Indiana.

Later, sometime in the late 90's, Gerry asked Beverly to come for a visit for a brainstorming meeting. In a very short time, she had pretty much laid out the content and authors for the next two issues. There was some talk about Beverly's interest in becoming the editor, but Beverly graciously declined.

In 2008, in Vol. 5- Issue 3, Gerry Durnell wrote: "Beverly provided the lasting inspiration and insight that history, does not have to be a boring recitation of mere dates and facts; and that history was created by humans. Some were rascals, and others were brilliant, likeable folks such as you would like to have as friends. She wouldn't have it any other way."

I was always amazed by Bev's recall ability. Recently, in a conversation I had with Gerry, I mentioned this to him, and he said, "The reason Bev had such recall, is that, in addition to the fact that she studied automobile history, she also lived it." This also carried over in her personal life; she had the ability to recall conversations with individuals long after they had taken place. This was due to her true interest in what people had to say.

Even with the workload she had at A.Q., Bev still found time for other projects. That was how Bev was. There was always time for another person or project; she just worked longer hours. Other projects that Bev worked with included:

Harry N. Abrams, New York, on Peter Helck's book, *Automotive Art, World Book Encyclopedia,* Chicago, Illinois; contributing writer/ editor for "Automobile" section *Encyclopedia dell'Automobile*, Turin Italy; contributing editor for the U.S seven-volume Italian encyclopedia;

Bev also wrote a four-section history of the development of the American automobile industry, in addition to 16 articles about individual American automobiles. She served as reader/advisor for E.P. Dutton, Inc., New York, for books originating in England, and was advisor on calendar subjects and a copywriter for Joseph Hoover & Sons, Philadelphia, Pennsylvania.

Bev also designed a poster for the 1980 Hoosier Auto Show, held at the Indy 500 race track; and was appointed a judge for the event. James Hoggatt, Jr., of Indianapolis, said: "The nicest thing happened at the Hoosier Auto Show & Swap Meet....her name was Beverly."

Max Walters, a reporter for the *Gainesville News Examiner*, wrote: "Among the visiting notables for the

Hoosier Auto Show, will be Beverly Rae Kimes, Editor of Automobile Quarterly.

Beverly became a member of The Society of Automobile Historians in November of 1980. She served on the Board until she was elected President, in January of 1988. She didn't serve a full two-year term, since she was able to affect a change in the S.A.H. year.

At the time, the Society worked on a calendar year and changed to a fiscal year (October through September). This was a good change, since their Annual Board Meeting and awards banquet could then be conducted in October, during the same time as the Annual Antique Automobile Meet at Hershey, Pennsylvania. Most of the members would be attending the car meet, so it made attending meeting much easier. Bev also changed the annual spring meeting, from its long-time place in Philadelphia, to be held each spring at locations all over the U.S. This would give members, all over the country, an opportunity to attend a S.A.H. meeting.

Bev was also instrumental in getting a new event underway: The Silent Auction. Members would donate automotive materials to the Society which would be cataloged and offered to the membership as a list of items to bid on. The chore of organizing the auction was done by Beverly, in the beginning, and was later turned over to a committee to do. The proceeds went to the Society for operations expenses. In 2002, she was given a Certificate

of Appreciation from former Society President, Leroy Cole.

From 1980 until 2007, Beverly spent a lot of time at the podium announcing the winners and giving out awards, as well as receiving awards. During that time, she would be called to receive awards fourteen times. In addition to the Cugnot and Benz

Beverly at the check-in table, 1998

awards, she also received the Society's highest honor: The Friend of Automotive

58

History Award which read:
"In recognition of her dedication and significant contributions to the cause of Automotive History."

Beverly at the
podium, 2001

At the annual meeting's, her favorite place to be was at the check-in table. She said it was a way to get a chance to meet and greet all the members attending the Annual Banquet.

Beverly at work in her
new office, the kitchen
at 215 East 80th Street

After leaving *Automobile Quarterly*, her only other office, would be at 215, Apt LB, East 80th Street. When I first met her, her office was in the kitchen. She had covered the stove-top, for more filing space, and said that she often thought that she should get rid of the oven to hold pendaflex files. (Beverly didn't cook much, and that made good sense to her.) I, however, liked to cook very much (which she thought was a good thing), so the oven didn't get converted; and the files had to be removed from time to time.

Bev's new work space in the
study, with her Automotive Library

When she was finally pressured into the computer age, her work area moved to the study and to a proper desk. At the onset of the second book for the Classic Car Club, the club said that taking a manuscript from written to computer was very expensive; they would prefer that she do it on a computer. The club purchased the computer and printer, as well as all other start-up supplies. (This also included her

Bev with Jerri, the cat

computer training.) She had several computer teachers up to the apartment for lessons and support. The last and the best, was Mark Deutsch, who lived   in the same building. It was also very convenient, since he was able to respond to any and all of her computer needs in a short time. This need decreased quite a bit, as she became more familiar with computers.

Bev also bought two laptops; one to use in the bedroom, and a second one to take back and forth to Matamoras, so that she was never without one. She advanced quickly, and was very happy to have moved into the computer age. The second book for the Classic Car Club was done in half the time as it would have been, if it were a written manuscript, and much cheaper to publish. All of her writings and future books were produced quicker from this time on.

Chapter 5:
Beverly goes Freelance

Since she didn't have a position lined up when she resigned from *Automobile Quarterly*, Bev was quite concerned about her future. She had prepared a very

detailed resume, to be sent out for prospective employment; however, she never had to use it. In addition to the job as Editor of the Classic Car Club of America, she wrote ten books, did the editing for two others, and was a regular contributing writer to several magazines. She had more offers of works to do, than she would ever have time for.

Beverly and me, with Fred Roe, friend, fellow historian and author of "Duesenberg, The Persuit of Perfection."

One project that carried over from A.Q., and needed to be completed, was a Biography on Rene Dreyfus. (Bev considered Rene like a second father). Dreyfus had been a Grand Prix race driver and became Race Champion of France in 1938. On special leave from the French Army, he came to race at the 1939 Indianapolis 500

to promote good will for France. While he was in the U.S., Germany invaded Paris, leaving Rene stranded. He joined the U.S Army, and after the war, opened a restaurant, Le Chanteclair, in New York City. He brought his brother, Maurice, sister, Susan, and niece, Nicole, over from France to work in

Beverly and Rene, in his apartment in Queens, 1980

the restaurant. Le Chanteclair became an international watering hole for any and all race drivers, as well as race fans, until it changed ownership in 1980. Rene had a large collection of photographs of race drivers on the walls of

Beverly, Elio and Rene in Elio's Restaurant on Queens Blvd. in 1988

the restaurant, which he donated to the Taladaga Motor Speedway, when the restaurant closed.

While still at *Automobile Quarterly*, Beverly and Rene spent many Sunday afternoons and evenings talking and recording his recollections. This time was always followed by a late dinner at one of the local restaurants in Queens. In 1980, Rene was invited to be a guest of honor at the 50th Anniversary of his win of the 1930 Grand Prix of Monaco. He invited Beverly to be his guest. She travelled with Maurice and Rene to Monaco, and over a three-week excursion, was able to make it a very extensive visit to all the places that

Beverly and Rene while on their trip to France in 1980

Rene had raced. The highlight of the trip for Bev was a visit to one of Rene's racing friends, Enzo Ferrari, Bev said "I didn't know if I should genuflect or what!"

Rene's last official work with racing was as manager for Team Lotus in the late 1950's. One of the armature drivers was Walter Cronkite, who wrote the forward to the book, *My Two Lives from Race Driver to Restaurateur,*

Walter Cronkite and Beverly speaking at Rene's Memorial Services

which was published in 1983. To formally acknowledge having the honor of him writing the forward, Beverly and Rene had gone to lunch with Walter. Bev told me that she was quite excited to have the chance to meet such a famous personality, and one of her favorite anchor newsmen.

My Two Lives was the recipient of the 1984 Society of Automotive Historians Cunot Award, for Best Book of 1983, as well as the Thomas Mckean Memorial Cup for most significant original research, awarded by the Antique Automobile Club.

1986, Chet Krause Beverly and Austie Clark with their awards for "The Standard Catalog of American Cars 1805 to 1942"

Her second book as a freelance writer was a huge undertaking, *The Standard Catalog of American Cars, 1805 to 1942*. She co-authored the book with Henry Austin Clark, Jr. It was a volume of over 1500 pages and over 5000 listings of American automobiles. It included everything from listings of single efforts to mass manufacturers. At the onset, Bev asked if I would do the filing of research for her, and I said that I would. This job started out to be light; however, by the time the first edition was done, there were ten banker boxes of research materials. There were two other editions that Beverly was involved in, and each one contained new listings and another three banker boxes. For the forth edition, she was not consulted. "Too bad," she had said, since she had gathered a few more listings which would have added more to the history of the automobile. The folder of information is still in her research materials; they are now in the care of The Society of Automotive Historians and housed at the Auburn, Cord, Duesenburg Museum in Auburn Indiana. These files can be accessed by anyone doing automotive research.

Over the years, the *Standard Catalog of American Cars,* has become a "must read" for libraries and automobile enthusiasts the world over. This project was the grand vision of Chert Krause, publisher of Krause Publications, and was published in 1985. The catalog received two major awards: The Society of Automotive Historians Cugnot for Outstanding book of 1985, and the Thomas McKean Memorial Cup for most significant original research, from The Antique Automobile Club. When first published, the catalog price was under $40.00. On the current market, its sells for anywhere from $350.00 to $695.00

Stan Grayson, a former collogue and lifetime friend, said: "While doing my final fact-checking for my book on stationary engines, I referred to The *Standard Catalog,* and sure enough, I was able to find the facts. Bev had managed to so accurately record the many instances when long ago entrepreneurs had morphed from marine engine builders to automobile builders (or vice versa), and what became of them. Names, dates, places – all were there."

Beverly, Jon Lee, Katie Robbins and Bob Joint, at the registration table, Metro Grand Classic 2004

When asked about the time it took to write the catalog, Bev said "The history of the automobile is a can of worms, that would make any self-respecting bilateral invertebrate blanch."

Just a short time after becoming a freelance writer, Bev was contacted by Katie Robbins, who was then President of The Classic Car Club of America. Robbins inquired if Beverly would like to be the new editor of the club's publications. This consisted of getting out four magazines, and assisting with eight bulletins per year. Bev accepted the position, and her first contact with the club, as editor, was when she attended a Grand Classic event in Baltimore, Maryland in July of 1981.

During the event, on Friday evening, there was a bus trip down to the Inner Harbor for cocktails and dinner. Beverly was the last person to board the bus, and, (as she told me the next day), she was a little embarrassed; she had timed how long it would take from her room to the bus, since she did not want to be early. What she didn't know is that Classic Car Club members tend to be early, when it involves food and drink.

The only seat left on the bus was next to me. By the time the evening was over, we had become somewhat acquainted. I was single, and so was she; we continued to get more acquainted over the weekend. She invited me to come into New York for dinner, the following weekend, and by the time the evening was over, we both had decided to see each other on a regular basis. I believe, and I'm reasonably sure Beverly would agree, that the real success of our relationship was our very similar up-bringing,

  as well as our ability to support each other in all of our needs. Bev was sort of shy, and never forgot her roots.

Bev and I went to Baltimore in 1991 and again for a C.C.C.A. Grand Classic in 1997.

She sure could have been very uppity, given the success that she had achieved, but that was not her style. She was simply, Bev, through and through.

Shortly into our relationship, Bev called me at work one day and said: "How would you feel if a little bundle of joy were to come into our lives?" Needless to say, I was a little stunned. She left me hang only briefly, and then she said, "This lovely stray cat has been coming to the Clark's back door for some time, and they can't keep it, because Austie is allergic to cats. Can we please keep it?" Of course I said, yes, and we had our first pet, Jerry. Shortly afterwards, Bev found out that she, too, was allergic to cats. "I will take shots for the rest of my life, if need be," she said, "before I will give up Jerry." After taking shots for a short time, her allergies went away; and over time, we got four more cats. They were pairs: Ralph and Trixie, Oscar and Maggie. (Oscar is still with me.)

Bev and I spent three years together and we married on July 6th 1984.

Shortly after taking the job at the Classic Car Club, Bev was asked if she would take over the bulletin (since the level of both content and interest were very low), and she did. The quality of content and interest increased greatly over the years. It came to be, that the bulletin was more anticipated by the members, than the magazine. It had come from a four-page fold-out, to average more than 32 pages per issue. Bev created various new columns, and there was a whole lot more information for the members to consume and reply to.

At this point, I would like to mention two of her long-time proof readers (who did a lot of reading); Joe Malaney, of Sarasota, Florida, and Matt Sonfield of Oyster Bay, New York. Both were also Classic Car Club members.

Both of the publications were done by cut-and-paste method from start to finish. (For those that are not familiar with this term, cut-and-paste means, literally, just that. The text and photographs are cut out and glued or taped to lay-out sheets.) This was a quite unusual, since many authors and editors of publications and books had long since gone over to using computers. In 2008, when I approached Stan Grayson (a colleague) to assume temporary charge of the Classic Car Club Publications, until Beverly could be released from the hospital, he said, "I'm very busy with my own projects and I'm not sure I have the time." After a little more pleading on my part, however, he agreed to do this. Had it not been for the sake of Beverly, I'm sure he wouldn't have. Beverly had the next issue of the magazine laid out. When I sent it to Stan, his response was, "God, she is still doing cut-and-paste." When she was asked, why she didn't use a computer, to this she would reply, " The only reason I got a typewriter was because I couldn't find a quill that I liked." Beverly preferred to be low tech. This would change later, however, and when it did, she came to realize the computer was a wonderful tool.

As you must know by now, Beverly always strived for perfection. Since, on my first attempt to help, I put down a photograph that was a little crooked, I was dismissed from any further help of this nature. I did, however, attain the title of research and file assistant, which I did for the rest of Bev's life.

66

Bev wrote two books for the Classic Car Club. The first was called *The Classic Car*. This book was about the members' cars, and their reasons for owning them. The second book, *The Classic Era*, featured the members' cars, but was written as a history of the times — starting in the mid-twenties and ending in the mid-forties. For this book, she received two major awards: The Cugnot, for Outstanding book in the English language, 2001 from the Society of Automotive Historians, and the 2001 Thomas McKean Memorial Cup, for the most significant original research, from the Antique Automobile Club. The classic car publications received several Golden Quill awards from the *Old Cars Weekly* publication.

Beverly was awarded the Classic Car Club of America, Citation for Distinguished Service in 1991, and was presented with a large hard bound book at the 50th Anniversary Meeting in 2002.

Dick Gold, President of the Classic Car Club of America, presented Beverly with the Distinguished Service Award,1991

Beverly receiving the "Sprirt of St. Louis Award from Fred Guyton

Beverly being presented with Book, by Fred Guyton in 2002

On left, Beverly and Gene Perkins at a party given by Mr. and Mrs. Joe Falladori

67

It contained 69 testimonials letters from all walks of her life. This was spearheaded by friend and fellow club member George Tissin, of Scottsdale, Arizona.

In 1991, Gene Perkins, President of The Classic Car Club, wrote: "There can never be enough words of extreme gratitude and appreciation extended to you for the beautiful end — product you gave us all — *The Classic Car Book*. What a job! What a trying experience! You had to work with all of us Club members. How can we ever begin to say Thank You enough? Your talent, your efforts, and your many hours of dedication have given us all a great treasure that we will be enjoying for many years to come."

In 1994, Member Jim Balfour wrote: "Her talent in the Automotive History Field is unparalleled, and we love her." In 2008, after her passing, The Classic Car Club of America created a National Award in her name to be given annually, to an outstanding Regional Editor.

The following are other written works by Beverly as a freelance writer. *The Star and the Laurel.* She was contacted by Leo Levien, Mercedes of North America, and asked if she would write a hundred-year history of Daimler, Mercedes and Benz. When she accepted the project, she and Leo made an extended trip to Stuttgart Germany. The trip allowed her to do research, and for Leo to visit with the people at Mercedes. Since she did not speak or read German, Bev would simply gather materials about names and places she had already known. Her knowledge, at that point, came from doing the book on Rene Dreyfus, and articles written for *Star Magazine*, the official publication of the American Mercedes Club.

Her knowledge also came from research on German race drivers and races on the continent, as well as early Vanderbuilt races on Long Island, New York. These races were originally promoted by Willy K. Vanderbuilt, who was a great promoter of the automobile in the early 1900's. He also owned and raced early American Mercedes.

68

When Bev arrived back home from her trip, she contacted a good friend, Christa Ficken, to translate the gathered materials. Christa, of West Babylon New York, was born and raised in Germany, and came to the United States when she married her husband David, who had been in the U.S. Navy. Along with this information and additional research on the American Mercedes from the early 1900's, Bev was able to write the *Centennial History*, published in 1986. In 1987, she received the Society of Automotive Historians Cunot Award for Best Book in 1986, and the Thomas Memorial Cup from the Antique Automobile Club, for most significant original research.

Beverly was a contributing writer to *Star Magazine* for quite a few years, and had a great working relationship with the editor, Frank Barrett. This stopped when the Mercedes Club interests moved into the more modern years, and members had no further interest in what happened in the early years.

One article of dual interest, was a transcontinental trip from New York to San Francisco, California by Emily Post (before she became known as 'the' Emily Post.) Emily had been recently divorced, and entered into a deal with a New York newspaper to make this trip and report back every week about her adventures. She made the trip in a 1907 Mercedes, which was loaded with all kinds of things she thought were necessary for the trip, including china, silverware and linens. By the time they had reached Albany three days later, however, she decided to lighten the load. The transcontinental trip took about two months; and she sent weekly reports about the trials and hardships of the journey. Shortly afterwards, she gained notoriety as 'the' Emily Post.

Beverly thought this story was worthy of a screenplay, and she and neighbor, Pat Erie, worked on this, on a weekly basis, for over a year. The project was coming along nicely, but was never completed. Both women really had such fun with this project. When Bev passed away, I gave the uncompleted screenplay to Pat. Most likely, it will never be completed; but for Pat, it will forever be a very

69

good memory of Bev for years to come.

The following was a comment of Smith Hempstone Oliver, regarding one article Bev wrote in *Star Magazine:* "I should like to let you know how thoroughly I am enjoying Beverly Rae Kime's article on Manfred von Brauchitsch. How she writes so well, on so many unrelated automotive subjects, I have never been able to fathom. I constantly refer to her definitive book, *Standard Catalog of American Cars 1805–1942,* and always find it informative. May she long continue to share her knowledge with us poor mortals!"

Pioneers, Engineers and Scoundrels, The Dawn of The Automobile in America, is a very definitive history of the industry and the people. Bev said, "I have been writing this book in bits and pieces for four decades, and it's my most favorite book." We had a lot of fun together, coming up with titles for the chapters, since they set the mood for each and every chapter. I always enjoyed helping with research, proofreading, and titles. In later years, armed with written instruction which she would provide for me, I would go to the library to look up things for her. The writing of *Scoundrels* was set aside about three times, to do other work, including two books for The Classic Car Club and magazine articles. *Scoundrels* received the 2006 Society of Automotive Historians Cunot Award for Best Book of 2005.

At the request of Sandra Kasky, Manager of the Concours, Bev wrote the book, *Pebble Beach, Concours d! Elegance, The First 50 Years.*

Speed, Style and Grace, a book about Ralph Lauren's automobile collection, was done in conjunction with his collection being put on display at the Museum of Fine Arts in Boston. Initially, it was thought that this exhibit would not draw much interest, but the people who had proposed the exhibit were of another opinion. Their opinion proved to be correct, and the exhibit drew big crowds. I believe that it was among the largest draw of all exhibits. The book was co-authored with Winston Goodfellow, from Carmel Ca. Winston, who chronicled the later exotic cars; Beverly did the history on the post-war automobiles. The book was a hit, and sold a lot of copies. If my memory serves me correctly, Mr. Lauren purchased 10,000 copies right off of the press.

Marr, Buick's Amazing Engineer; was a book that had been started by Richard P. Scharchburg, a long time colleague, and a Thompson professor of Industrial History. Scharchburg had gathered research and files, which were current up to the turn of the last century, but never started the writing. When he passed away, Bev was asked by Leroy Cole, a long-time friend of both her and Richard, to consider taking over the project. Beverly said to me, "Jim, I would very much like to do this book, but I can't without your help." (The book was full of mechanical terms and information that I knew more about than Bev did.) I said I would. In addition to the material that Scharchburg had gathered, there was a lot more information waiting in Signal Mountain, Tennessee, from Bill Close (who was married to Marr's granddaughter, Sarah).

There was also information from Dan Williams, a relative interested in aviation, who supplied information on Marr's aviation ventures. Walter L. Marr was a brilliant engineer, and did a lot of really good projects during his tenure at Buick. Prior to going to work for Buick, He had also engineered and built the Marr Car. The materials supplied by Bill Close were just great, and included correspondence from a lot of the people involved with automobiles at the time. They included Henry Ford, William Crapo Durant, Walter P. Chrysler, Charles W. Nash, David Buick and others.

This correspondence was really interesting and informative; it also made Bev and I feel like we were there at the time they were written. Bill had restored the Marr Car, as well as the one and only Marr Cycle Car. (To this day, they are still in the Marr family, under the care of Bill's son, Barton.) In 1916, Marr designed two Buick V/12 engines that were put into production chassis. One went to Marr, the other, to Walter P. Chrysler. (The Marr V/12 Buick is also still in the Marr family, in the care of Paul Marr.)

Bev also co-wrote *The Pursuit of Uncommon Excellence*, a biography on Otis Chandler, publisher of the *Los Angeles Times Newspaper*, with writer, Randy Leffingwell. This book had been started, but was having problems. Those involved were not up to the expectations of Bettina Chandler, Otis' wife, who contacted Beverly and asked her to take over and help finish the book. I knew Otis, personally. He was quite a collector of automobiles and motorcycles, and a supporter of the motorcycle exhibit at the Guggenheim Museum in New York City. There were 'naysayers' that said the exhibit was not a good idea, but they were proven wrong. The motorcycle exhibit was the most successful exhibit in the history of the Guggenheim.

One day, Bev and I went to see the motorcycle exhibit, and we counted motorcycles from 8 different states, parked in the front of the museum. Bev also wrote a tribute to Otis, for the Inaugural Rocky Mountain Concours d' Elegance. When it came to automobiles and motorcycles, Otis only collected the best of the best.

There are two other articles that I think are worthy of mention:
One article, written for *Road and Track* in November of 1989, was about a 1908 American LaFrance Roadster. Figgie International owned American La France, at the time. Our restoration company did a complete restoration on this roadster, and as far as we knew, it was the only example that exists. (American LaFrance was a manufacturer of firefighting equipment, but developed some automobiles on request.)

In response to this article, Gary L. Hoedmaker, an art director from Nutley New Jersey, wrote, " Ms. Kimes' piece of reportage in the current issue (December 1989) of *Road and Track* represents writing in its highest form. The choice of words is impeccable; the structure, the flow, the imagery. They are altogether human, warm. In short, reading her prose is as joyful as listening to Tchaikovsky or Gershwin ... or an un-muffled 1957 Ferrari Testa Rossa."

The second article of note was a story about the legendary 1970 Plymouth Super Bird that was done for *Special Interest Auto Magazine*. The article appeared in the magazine, in August 1987. It was written about Richard (King) Petty, in a Shakespearian theme. Richard had left Chrysler to race Fords, but was brought back to the Chrysler fold by the Superbird. He only raced the Superbird for one season, but it was a very good year for Chrysler and Petty. So good, that NASCAR wouldn't allow the car to race the following year, unless it was de-tuned. So, Richard put his Superbird in his museum; and that was that. The car that was photographed for this article, was one of our restorations, and belongs to Gilbert Jacobs of Landing, New Jersey.

Bev also edited two biographies. The first was *W. Dorwin Teague, Industrial Designer, and the Artist as Engineer*. Beverly met Dorwin (as he preferred to be addressed), through *Automobile Quarterly*. Dorwin was

responsible for the entire body designs for the Marmon V/16 automobiles from the early 1930's.

Beverly and Dorwin, on one of our many visits to see him

During the time that they were working together on the book, Bev and I made quite a few trips to Nyack, New York. All these visits concluded by Dorwin taking us out for lunch at his favorite eateries in the area. Following the publication of his book, Dorwin visited the Concours of the Eastern United States, Pebble Beach, Greenwich and Amelia Island — all to revisit his creations (the Marmon V/16's). He was well received by the Councours, and by the owners that had their Marmons on display. The last couple of visits that we had with Dorwin, it became obvious to Bev and me that he was becoming a little weak of mind, and quite forgetful. In fact, our concern was that he would go somewhere, and not remember how to get back. With this in mind, we called his son; Harry, who lived in Aspen, Colorado, and voiced our concerns. Harry very quickly moved his dad to Aspen, in 2003. In April, 2004, Bev got a call from Harry, saying that Dorwin was failing; so, Bev made a trip to

Aspen to visit one last time with him. He passed away a short time later.

The second book that Bev edited was *Equations of Motion*, by W.F. Milliken. Bill Milliken graduated from M.I.T in 1944, and went into aircraft stabilization. Much later, Bill started a company with his son Doug, dealing with aerodynamics and the stabilization of automobiles. Bill was also an amateur racecar driver. Bill raced a Bugatti at the inaugural Vintage race at Watkins Glen, New York, and flipped it on a turn. (He now has the honor of having that corner named after him.) Bill raced this automobile for quite a few years, and at one time, converted it to four-wheel-drive to do the Hill Climb at Pikes Peak, Colorado.

Bill Milliken and son at Watkins Glen, in Bill's "Miller Special"

Beverly's taping of the "History of Packard," at our good friend Tom Kerr's Carriage House.

Beverly also made appearances on two Automobile History segments of the History Channel. One segment concerned the early years of the automobile, the second, was about the Packard automobile. The early years segment was filmed at our restoration shop, with Bev seated in front of her 1908 Sears. For the second segment, we traveled to Warren, Ohio, where the Packard Motor Car Company was founded. This segment was also being done in conjunction with the 100th Anniversary Celebration by the Packard Automobile Club. In a letter to Bev from Jim Pearsall of Zarephath, New Jersey, he wrote: "Dear Bev; We watched the History Channel Packard program on Christmas Eve, and were so surprised and immensely happy to see and hear you having such a prominent part. That made the whole thing so wonderful! I had no idea that you were going to play a significant part."

Bev with Tom Kerr in Hersey, circa 2000

In the early years, Beverly also did all the tablet writing, for each car on display in the Miles Collier

Beverly on the show field at Pebble Beach, as an Honorary Judge

Automobile Museum in Naples, Florida. Beverly and I were invited to attend the museum pre-opening black tie affair. It started out very formal, but a little later in the evening, as the band played on, all ties, jackets and the ladies' shoes were off. It turned out to be a really fun party.

On many occasions, Bev was also invited to be Grand Marshal or Honorary Judge and guest speaker at various Automobile Shows and Concours. The two most notable, were the Pebble Beach Concours d'Elegance, and Concours d'Elegance of the Eastern United States. She was Grand Marshal of the Concours d'Elegance of the Eastern United States for 14 years.

Bev with Denise McLuggage, race driver, journalist and photographer, along with reknown automobile designer, Signore Scaglietti

Beverly's first appearance at the Eastern United States Concours d' Elegance, as Grand Marshal in 1990, was at the Berks County Campus of Penn State, in Reading, Pennsylvania. It was a very nice sunny day, and other than a couple of cars being out of order (which created a little disorder in her presentation), the day went very well.

In 1996, the Eastern United States Concours moved to Lehigh University in Bethlehem, Pennsylvania, and remained there until 2007. During this period in time, her main contacts were Martha Cusimano, Executive Director and her husband Jim. In a note written on December 13, 2000, Martha wrote, "Sparkle and shine in the face of darkness. I remember so many times when you chose to sparkle and shine in the face of the darkness of health crises and other tough times, personally and for the show. As you enjoy this millennium gift from Jim and me, think of that motto and enjoy the knowledge that you have contributed so much to the success of the show. You are, indeed, our star and best of all, our friend."

The following is from a 1996 New York Auto Show press release:
"The show will officially open with a historic cavalcade of cars parade, Saturday, April 6 at 10 a.m. Ms. Kimes will be stationed at the entrance to the Crystal Palace on 11th Avenue, to provide commentary." In that commentary, Bev said: "It is a delight to help celebrate the industry that has had such a dramatic impact on life in

Outside with Beverly, Fred Cantor, Martha Cusimano and radio personality "Cousin Brucie" Marrow

America. The Automobile freed us to enjoy our beautiful country, in a way that was never possible in the nineteenth century. It put wheels to Americans' dreams, and gave new meaning to freedom of movement. Simply put, it changed the way we live." Beverly was joined at the podium by Mayor Rudolph Giuliani, and WCBS oldies FM radio personality "Cousin Brucie" Marrow. Fred Cantor, chairperson of the car selection committee, organized a Concours display at the location, to promote the Concours and its new location at Lehigh University.

Bev, inside with Mayor Giuliani, Fred Cantor and Martha Cusimano

As Grand marshal of the Concours d'Elegance, Bev wrote an article that appeared in the June 12, 1996, issue of *Old Cars Weekly*: "Of all of mankind's modern inventions, the automobile is the most important...most probably. The qualifier has been added, only to assuage those who might argue for the telephone, television or toaster oven. In terms of social impact, however, there is no contest. Once the world was put on wheels, nothing was ever the same again."

Another one of her frequent quotes was: "Until the

day that we are beamed from place to place like in Star Trek, we are going to be in love with the automobile."

Beverly goes for a spin, in a 1913 Triumph Type C Roadster McWicker Side Car, belonging to Pepe and Claudia Merrick of Covington LA

Beverly's mission was to share her love of automobile history with the rest of the planet. She said, "No other industry, no other entity, combines the sparkling cast of unforgettable characters, the drama, the comedy, the tragedy, the whole spectrum of life, like the saga of how the world was put on wheels."

Beverly would spend hours preparing her notes for each and every car that would be at the Concours. Each card would have the history of the car, as well as some interesting facts about what was going on when each was made. And, as each car made its way to the reviewing stand, the people would be properly welcomed and introduced.

On the occasions that she knew the owners, personally, she would refer to them as my friends," and speak of them in a personal way. All of the participants did the drive-by. Then later in the day, the

Beverly doing her thing around circa late 90's

award winners would make another pass to accept their award. This made the Concours very popular; and people would come quite a distance with their cars to be a part of show. In one instance, when a very elegant Stutz was in front of the reviewing stand, Bev said, *"Ain't Misbehaving"* was a popular tune when this car was new. This car, however, you could misbehave in!"

One award winner, Chet Doughman from Wisconsin, wrote:
"Dear Ms. Kimes; I want you to know how much I appreciate the chance to meet you, and shake that hand

that penned so many outstanding books and feature stories. As you may remember, the good folks at the Bethlehem Concours had our 1902 Rambler out of sequence at the award parade, so I did not hear what award it had won. After I parked around the rear, my wife, JoAnn, came running up and told me she had spoken to you, and it would all right to stop by and say hello. What good news this was. I hurried to the big tent and made your acquaintance — what a thrill. We then loaded the trailer and headed for home. When we had driven about twenty miles, I asked JoAnn to open the box and see if there was any indication as to what the trophy might be for. We were both just elated to find that we had won the Grand Marshal's Award. Of all the AACA, HCC and other awards that the old Rambler has won, this one is the best. It's the seal of approval from America's foremost antique automobile authority — and it's very special to me. Again, thank you for choosing the 02 Rambler and long-awaited opportunity to meet you."

The people that made up the audience came back year after year, just to listen to Bev's commentary. Bev always told well informed histories and information that made each commentary entertaining, all presented in a light hearted manner. I often called her the Pied Piper, because she had the same effect on people as the one in legends.

During the A.C.D. Spring Meet in 2000, I was approached by Roe Bogart to make sure that we planned to return to Auburn for the Annual Fall Meet. (Evidently, I was to receive an award at that time.) On Sunday morning, as we left to attend the Fall Meet banquet, Bev said to me, "Make sure you look surprised." Well, it turned out to be Bev,who was surprised. She was presented with the award for A. C. D. Woman of the Year.

A letter from Tom Bolinbaugh of 333 East 80th St, New York City:
"Dear Ms. Kimes; As a regular spectator at Redding, I must tell you how marvelous it was to have you back this year as Grand Marshal. Your knowledge, witty and fast

78

Bev's surprised by her award announcement; behind Bev: Stan Gilliland, Past A.C.D. President

On the way to the podium; Next to Bev: Rick Zieger, A.C.D. President

Bev receives the Woman of the Year Award from Nettie Van-Ausdal-Etter

paced commentary is without equal and sets Redding apart from other Concours."

Ellen M. Huyett (General Chair Person of the Concours), wrote:
"Dear Beverly & Jim; My personal thanks for making such an overwhelming effort to participate in our Concours. As usual, Beverly, I thoroughly enjoyed every minute of your witty commentary. You make the cars come alive! Your support of our Concours is greatly appreciated. Thank you also for proofing the car portion of the program — what a help!"

The one and only thing that was very disruptive and stressful for Bev, was if the cars got out of order for the drive-by. In some cases, there would be multiples of the same make and year. This made it difficult, if not impossible; to announce the cars in their proper order, but then; thankfully, along came Pete Cheplick. Pete handled the order of cars, and after he took over, I don't remember a single glitch in the line as they came forward. He would manage the order from the tent, using walkie-talkies to talk to volunteers stationed on the field and on the line. If, for some reason, a car failed to make the drive-by, this information was relayed to Pete, and then to Beverly.

For her last two years with the Concours, Beverly was assisted by Bill Rothermel, who had joined the

Concours as a judge in 1996. Bill was also a member of the car selection committee, and co-anchor for the Parade of Cars. Bill would do the segments for special events for more contemporary cars. As Bev told Bill, "You are more qualified to do these than I."

Beverly's last Concour was 2005. She was picked up in New York, by limousine, on Saturday June 18, and returned late in the day on Sunday. I went outside to help her from the limousine to the apartment. She was totally exhausted, and said to me, "This has to be my last time; I just don't have the stamina or energy to do this anymore." I was just heartbroken to see her this way, and to

Bill Rothermel, who assisted Bev for special events

think that she was forced, by health issues, to give up another thing that she really loved to do.

Bill took over as Grand Marshal in 2006. Bill credits Bev as being his mentor. When he suceeded her as Grand Marshal, he was quick to point out: "I ain't no Bev Kimes." I think Bev was happy about her successor; and when I attended the 2009 Concours to present the 1st annual award in Beverly's name, I thought he did an admirable job of announcing the Concoures. The annual award, in Beverly's memory, went to the Best Brass-Era Car attending the show.

Bill has a lot of interest in cars, from classics to muscle cars, Post War American cars, European sports cars and automobile racing of all kinds. Bill is also a freelance writer, contributing to various national and international and club publications. He is a contributing editor for both the Antique Automobile Club of America Museum newsletter, and *Auto Events Magazine*. Although he has all this in his background, he still credits Bev as his mentor. He has told me more than one time, that he has advanced his level of writing by having known Bev, and the help she offered to him. He has recently advanced to doing feature articles for *Automobile Quarterly*.

A letter from B. Daniel Dillard, another solid 'rock' to Bev at the Concours:

" Dear Beverly; It is the unanimous desire of the cabinet or the Concours d' Elegance of the Eastern United States, to designate you as our 2007 National Chairperson. Over the past 15 years, you have been one of the fundamental architects of our event's reputation and excellence. Despite our growing pains, and your own personal physical challenges, you have stuck with us — advising us, admonishing us, sharing your wealth of knowledge, and engaging personally with both our team and show enthusiasts. This has been an extraordinary gift, and one worthy of public recognition! We could do no better than to announce Beverly Rae Kimes as the National Honorary Chairperson of the Concours d' Elegance of the Eastern United States! Thank youfor your consideration of our request. We eagerly await your response".

Beverly responded saying, "Your generous letter has brightened my day, but I cannot accept your wonderful offer. My medical condition has taken a difficult turn and does not allow me to continue many of the things I have long enjoyed doing. Please know that my best wishes for the continuing success of the Concours and the Foundation's important work will be with you always. And my memories of this glorious event will ever burn brightly." Even without attending the event, she was, nonetheless, listed in the 2007 program as National Chairperson of the Concours d' Elegance of the Eastern United States.

It was an end to an era. It was such a shame that Beverly had to, again, give up something she enjoyed so much. When she passed away, I turned over all her research records for the Concours to Bill. I knew that these would be a great help to Bill for future Concours, and that Bev would have wanted it that way.

It is also worth noting that, during this time, Bev was also a board member and advisor to the following organizations: Museum of Transportation, Brookline, Massachusetts; Fredrick C. Crawford Auto-Aviation

81

Museum, Cleveland, Ohio; Automotive History Collection, Detroit, Michigan; Auburn-Cord-Duesenberg Museum, Auburn, Indiana; Saratoga Automobile Museum, Saratoga, New York; and The Rolls-Royce Foundation.

Chapter 6:
In the Classic Car Business

In 1982, I quit the job I had for over 15 years. I could no longer tolerate the person that I was working for.

Since Bev also disliked the person, she was not upset about this either. In fact, she said to me, after the fact, "Had you continued to work for that person, I'm not sure that our relationship would have lasted."

Sussex Motor & Coach Works, Branchville, N.J

In April of that year, we opened our own business: Sussex Motor & Coach Works in Branchville, New Jersey. It was a small place, and needed a lot of clearing and cleaning before we could even get started. Beverly didn't spend too much time at the business, since there were very little amenities or heat. Over the next couple of months, I learned that this building was considered a non-conforming use. In a non-conforming zone. It would be almost impossible to get variances to enlarge the building, and we would need more space than we had, if we were to grow and improve our business. In February of 1983, I crossed the river into Pennsylvania, and started to

look in Pike County for a more suitable building for our business. Finally, by June, I had found one.

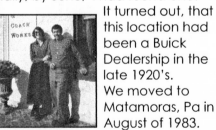

The location at 107 Ave, Matamoras, PA

It turned out, that this location had been a Buick Dealership in the late 1920's. We moved to Matamoras, Pa in August of 1983.

Beverly and me, circa late 80's

After we got somewhat settled, we engaged an attorney, Charles F. Lieberman, of Matamoras, to get the proper paper work done to form a sub-chapter S corporation for our business. Officers named were James H, Sr., President; James Jr., Vice President; and Beverly Rae (Kimes) Cox, Secretary and Treasurer. The next step, was to find an accountant. For this, we chose Edward J. Schafer, also of Matamoras. As treasurer, Beverly was the one to work with Ed. He turned out to be a very good choice, and he and Bev had an excellent working relationship for the next 24 years. At the time, we had to file three different tax returns: our business, Bev's business, and our joint personal return. She always did work-up sheets for each, regarding income, expenses and donations. With these, and minimal discussion, Ed would then work all this into a proper tax return.

Jim Jr. applying his skills in the shop

The beginning was a little rough. Although I had been around antique and classic cars and their owners for over 15 years, it would be three years before we started to get meaningful and major jobs. At the time we bought the building, there was a company that rented part of our space. This rent was enough to pay the mortgage. By the time the renter was leaving to relocate, we had grown to the point that we needed the space anyway; and our income could more than cover the loss of rent. We renovated the space vacated by the tenant and, by then, we had proper amenities and heat; as well as a small apartment in one corner off the office. Bev now spent a lot of time at the shop. She was the overseer of the paint, decorating, and decor, which she enjoyed.. When she was all caught up with paper work for our business, she would work on her own writing and editing. She also was spending as much time as she could, setting up her archive room, and doing research from her files. Once the room was orderly and completed to her satisfaction, she would often take visitors up to show them the archives.

We had bought a 10,000 square foot building, in Matamoras, Pa. It was home to Sussex Motor & Coach Works, our Antique and Classic Car restoration business. On an upper level, we had built a 24' x 30' room with shelves on two walls and file cabinets on another. The fourth wall had two large closets for storage of supplies and clothing. This would become Bev's Archives and storage area. I remember that it took two loads of a full-size pickup truck — the bed loaded to the top — to move the first group of historic research material from the apartment in New York, to Pennsylvania.

Beverly hard at work, doing the books, with her trusty helper, Ralph.

Our first complete restoration was a 1968 Shelby Mustang. At its first showing at a Shelby Club Spring National Meet, it was judged Best of Show over a field of 110 Shelby's, Cobra's, and Ford Boss Mustangs. Over the next 17 years, we would turn out many 100 point cars that would be judged Best in Class, Best of Show, and Class Winners at car club shows and Concours d' Elegance's throughout the country.

Over the years, our restoration shop would earn a stellar reputation for turning out high quality, show-worthy, and very road-worthy automobiles. My feeling had always been that every automobile we did, must be 100% dependable and road-worthy. Sussex Motor & Coach Works was among the top restoration shops in the country.

Ray, Beverly, Me and Grace

In early July of 1984, we headed west to Eagle River, Wisconsin to get married, the Ceremony took place July 6, on her parents' deck overlooking the lake. We were married by Pastor Richard Shout. My best man was Austie Clark, and Bev's Maid of Honor was her sister, Sharon. Others who attended that day were: Ray and Grace, Wally Clark, Pamela and Cullen, Sharon's children, Mrs. Shout, and our cat Jerry.

85

It was a very sunny, lovely day, and a very lovely simple ceremony, followed by cake and champagne. Afterward, we all went out that evening for a wedding dinner.

The whole wedding party

The following morning, we all set out for Iola, Wisconsin for our wedding weekend. We were going to attend the Iola Annual Old Car Show and Swap Meet. Where else would car people want to be? We were guests of Chet Krause, of Krause Publications, at his restored historic farmhouse. The weather for the whole weekend was just great, and we all enjoyed the weekend very much.

At the Iola Old Car Meet,
Grace, Austie, Bev and Sharon

From the beginning of our relationship, Bev took me to see plays on Broadway, off Broadway and off, off Broadway. This was something that she enjoyed very much, and was her first love.

We saw Glenn Close at The Manhattan Theater off Broadway in *The Singular Life Of Albert Dobbs,* long before most folks would know who she was. I can't tell you how many plays we saw from 1982 to 2006, but I can tell you there were many. In addition to seeing many Broadway shows, we were members of the Circle Repertory, Manhattan Theater Club and Lincoln Center.

For a few years after she arrived in New York, Beverly would often opt for standing room only tickets for plays, due to the lack of funds for full ticket prices. Nevertheless, she still got to do what she loved so much, which was to see plays. She had a collection of Play Bills going back to the mid sixties that filled more than ten binders, not to mention all the ones she had that weren't in binders. The last two years, we didn't go very much. It was not that we didn't want to go, but Bev's deteriorating

86

health meant we couldn't.

Over time, all the things that she enjoyed doing, would one by one had to be stopped. Although she never said much about it, I know that this saddened her, and in some cases, I'm sure that it also depressed her.

On the surface, she continued what she could do, and never complained about what she couldn't. The last couple years of her life were really bad for her. She had C.O.P.D., an enlarged heart, and chronic back pain problems. She tried everything available to try to find out the cause of her back pain, except (as she said) a voodoo doctor. "I would try that, if I knew where to find one."

The last suggestion from her doctors was to have exploratory back surgery, but she would have none of that. In 2006, she came down with a very bad case of the Shingles that never completely went away. Instead, it degenerated into Herpes, which was also quite painful.

A result of her early problems with her kidneys, Bev's kidneys failed back in 1993. After being on dialysis until May of 1997, she finally agreed to let her sister, Sharon, donate a kidney. (She really didn't have a choice, since dialysis was not doing much at the time.) Although Sharon was willing to donate a kidney from the day Bev's failed, Beverly felt strongly about not putting her sister at risk; she went on the waiting list for another donor.

The time she spent on dialysis was very painful, and a distressing time. She had only two good days each week; the rest were marginal. There were also problems with the Fistula, which was the tube for her dialysis treatment. It failed many times, during dialysis, which meant surgery every time it failed. Each time she had to have a catheter put into her chest, until the new Fistula matured.

The kidney transplant went very well, and gave Bev another ten years of life. To this date, February 17th 2010, Sharon has had no illness from donating the kidney. Her years of dialysis did not deter Bev from getting her work done, or making personal appearances at automobile events. She may not have been as fast, or gone as often as she would have liked, but nevertheless, she soldiered on. The really sad part was that the very thing that gave her life, would eventually take it away.

Over the years, the rejection medications Bev had to take for the kidney transplant slowly deteriorated her immune system. The last couple of years of her life, she could only get around with the aid of a cane, walker, or wheel chair. She continued her work, up to the last time she went in to the hospital, in late November of 2007.

On a personal level, our relationship was shared with automobiles and car clubs. We were members of the Classic Car Club (CCCA), The Auburn, Corrd, Duesenberg Club (ACD) and the Antique Automobile Club. Most of our time was spent with the CCCA and the ACD, attending

  various meets and doing driving tours.

Pacific Northwest caravan, Beverly and Al Mc Ewan, mid 90's

Beverly's thoughts on having her picture taken, Joe Falladori party,1990

Both Bev and I had been going to the Annual Antique Automobile Fall Meet in Hershey, Pennsylvania for years. She, with *Automobile Quarterly* to man their tent for sales and contacts, and me to promote classic and antique car restoration.

Beverly and me at a Packard meet, 1991

After we got together, we both enjoyed going to Hershey together. She would spend her time visiting the tents of the Classic Car Club and the Society of Automotive Historians; as well as spending some time at our tent, where she was often engaged in conversations with

88

fellow colleagues, car club members and admirers. Sometimes, she would even sell some of the items that we had brought to sell. I would spend part of my time looking for parts, or visiting with others.

Beverly attending to sales

Beverly in the motor home that we used later for the Hershey meet. The license plate on the table is a 1908 plate that had just been purchased for her Sears.

Beverly with Bill Davis, good friend and past president of The Classic Car Club, at the Classic Car tent at Hershey circa early 80's

We continued to make these annual trips, until 2007. It was not as easy to do after 1993, when her kidneys failed, and her C.O.P.D. got worse; but we continued to make the trip; the good times that we had, more than offset the hardships.

One visit to Hershey worth mentioning, was a trip that Bev made by herself, in 2003; while I stayed back

Sue Davis firing up a Stanley Steamer

home to run our antique store. She stayed at the Holiday Inn Express, where Sue Davis, of the Stanley Steamer Museum, was also staying. Sue, a long time friend to both of us, took Bev under her wing and looked out for her. She also drove Bev to the flea market field and back, two days in a row, in a turn-of-the century

89

Stanley Steamer. This was a true highlight and a real thrill to Bev, which she enjoyed so much.

At the 1987 Fall Meet, while visiting with friends, Pete and Joann McManus, and sharing a little food and drink, I mentioned I had once owned an Auburn, and had been thinking about perhaps buying another. About a week later, we got a note from Pete, saying: "I have an Auburn, that I have had it for ten years. I haven't done anything with it, and probably won't; perhaps you two might like to buy it." So, Bev and I made the trip to Chester, Pennsylvania, to see the car. When we pulled into the driveway, we could see the car in the back by their storage barn.

Bev and Pete with the Auburn, 1988

After trying to get it running, and doing a little road testing (which didn't amount to much), Pete went into the house. Bev and I remained outside. She had been taking all kinds of pictures, and was really enthusiastic about owning this car, but I wasn't. There were two reasons: (1) it was a much earlier model than I had in mind, and, (2) It needed a lot of work. I tried to point this all out to her, and asked her if she was sure we wanted this Auburn. She responded, that "we" did. (You see, this was more of her kind of car and, she said that the model year that I had in mind was "much to modern.")

So, we bought the 1930 Auburn Sport Sedan. When we went into the house, Bev wrote out a check. Pete looked at it and said to Bev: "Didn't we agree on a price? I think you have made the check for the wrong amount." Bev apologized and said, "In the all excitement of having the Auburn, I just wasn't thinking." We said our goodbyes, and started back for home, when I heard a car horn; I looked in my rear view mirror. There was Pete behind us, so I pull over and we had excitement number two: Bev had failed to sign the check!

The Auburn arrived at our restoration shop in the

Ralph, 1999

Beverly signing books
at The Grand
Experience at Hickory
Corners, MI

spring of 1988, and after considerable restoration repairs, it was about ready to go touring. After I got over the fact that the Auburn was older than my desires, (and I began to drive it), I began to really like it. It seemed to have a very good personality. Yes, cars do have gender and personalities to their owners. The name that Bev gave to our Auburn, was Ralph (after one of our beloved cats).

Over the next ten years, we put over 50,000 miles on Ralph; most of it very enjoyable, with only some minor glitches. These drives took us north as far as Sudbury, Canada, west as far as Kalamazoo, Michigan, south into the Virginias, and all the New England states on three different occasions. On one trip, we left Matamoras and drove to western Pennsylvania for an A.C.D. spring meet to spend a Memorial Day weekend. From there, we drove to Dearborn, MI. We spent two days in Dearborn, so Bev could stop in at the

Beverly at the
podium accepting
her induction into
the Hall of Fame

Automotive Hall of
Fame news story

Automotive History Collection, and visit with her old friend, Mark Patrick, who had been in charge of this collection for years.

We also paid a visit to the Automotive Hall of Fame, so that Bev could see, first hand, the listing of her induction. The following day, we drove up to Bloomfield Hills, to the Chrysler Museum, so that she could be interviewed about their history. After the interview, we headed west for Kalamazoo. We were there for two days and attended a car show: The Grand Experience, at the

91

Gilmore - Classic Car Club Museum at Hickory Corners. Then we headed back east. Total mileage for this trip, was just over 1,850 miles.

Most often, our Auburn was the oldest automobile on these driving tours. It made us feel proud that we could,  and did, drive an older car, while others elected to drive later model cars from the 1940's.

We were the hit of every service plaza where we stopped for a rest or fuel; particularly when tour buses with senior citizens would be there. In addition to all the comments and conversations, a lot of people wanted to have their picture taken with the car. Needless to say, these stops were often lengthy. It would be hard to put into words just how much Beverly enjoyed traveling in, and how proud she was, of Ralph. Suffice to say... extremely!

Ralph, in his retirement home, 2007

In 2007, we sold our building, and holding on to Ralph, ended up becoming a detriment. Added to this, was the fact that we didn't get to use Ralph much, since Bev's health problems had gotten worse. (There was very limited time that she could ride in it.) So, we both decided and agreed that if Ralph needed to have a new home, then the Auburn, Cord, Duesenberg Museum, in Auburn, Indiana, was where Ralph needed to be.

The museum is in the very building that was the original sales showroom for the company of the same name. Our Auburn would have originally been sold from that same showroom. Ralph had been extracted from an old wooden garage in Indianapolis, Indiana in the early 1960's. A previous owner from the early 1970's, Bill Greer of Indianapolis, thought that when the car was new, it might have been owned by a musician, (simply because in the 20's and 30's, musicians were known to drive these cars). When the interior was removed for restoration, drug paraphernalia was discovered in the right kick panel. (Oh, if only objects could tell tales.)

92

Bill and his wife, Carolyn, have been long-time friends. When Bill first took on the job of editor for The Stutz Car Club, he was encouraged and mentored by Beverly. He continues as editor to this day.

We donated Ralph to the museum, and he was picked up on a cold rainy night, in October of 2007. He was transported to his new home, by Blue Highways Transporting Company; in a nice enclosed trailer. The transporting company donated their services to transport the Auburn.

The Museum was very delighted to get Ralph. They didn't have much on display for the early years, and they loved the fact that he looked so good and was a very rare model. As far as I know, he's the only 1930, 8-125 Sport Sedan in existence. I have visited the museum twice, since Ralph was put on display in the main showroom by a large window. It makes me smile every time. Beverly never got a chance to visit the museum after Ralph went there, however, she did get to see a very nice photograph of him on the showroom floor.

In a previous chapter, I mentioned that Bev would eventually own a Sears Motor Buggy. Well, she owned one in 1988. Her third article for *Automobile Quarterly* was *Behold The High Wheeler — The Sears, For Instance*. The 1908 Sears that was used for photographs for the article, at that time, belong to Harold Craft from Oyster Bay, New York.

Bev spent time with Craft, to interview him as part of the story; since he had owned the Sears for 35 years. (I believe that he passed away in early 1988.) When I learned about his passing, I asked another friend, Marty Houghey, to let me know if his widow, Jessie, might sell the car; and one day, he called, and aid she might.

On a Monday morning, instead of leaving Manhattan for Pennsylvania, I went to visit Jessie. I told her that I wanted to buy the Sears for Beverly. She indicated that there were several people on Long Island that also wanted to buy it, but she would prefer that Beverly have it. So, we came to an agreement. Between Monday and Thursday, I went through a flurry of actions, to have the Sears paid for and delivered to our shop in Matamoras.

Beverly and her 1908 Sears Motor Buggy, 1988

On Thursday evening, before leaving to go to Manhattan, I had the Sears put in our paint spray booth. On Friday, when Bev and I arrived at the shop, I asked her to come in the back; there was something I want to show her. Before I opened the door to the booth, I said to her, "Now, whatever is in here is yours."

She gave me a look as if to say, "Another Mark 3 Lincoln" (since we already had three of them — as a matter of fact, our honeymoon car was our first Mark 3.) My son, James, Jr., was sitting in the seat, and he sounded the bulb horn. Boy, was Bev surprised! Her jaw dropped considerably. Having spent some time with the Sears, and having a love of early automobiles, made owning this car very special. The local newspaper even did a feature front page article on Beverly and her Sears, shortly after it arrived.

The Sears didn't get driven a lot of miles. Just how many, I can't say, since there wasn't anything to record them. We used the Sears somewhat locally, and took it to Long Island, twice, for the Long Island Old Car Club Annual Run for The Sea event, for cars made in 1914 or earlier.

Beverly and I arrive at a lunch stop, on The Run for The Sea, old car tour

Since the Sears didn't have much horse power (with its little two-cylinder engine), we always started early, ahead of the rest. We always got a standing ovation from the group at the lunch stop; since we were always last to arrive. We were also always

94

last to complete the day's run. That did not bother us.
We just enjoyed the drives in the Sears, and it always
         completed the runs.

         On a nice Saturday morning, we were driving along
Beach Road in the Hampton's, and off in the distance, we
saw a young lady out in a corral, riding a horse. The
modern cars that were passing by, did not faze the horse,
but as soon as we got within range of sight or sound, the
horse began to rear up and was quite disturbed. Perhaps
his ancestors passed down the legend of the horseless
carriage! At any rate, Beverly said, "This makes me so
happy; after all the years of reading and writing about
how early automobiles affected horses, I have finally
seen it, firsthand."

         When we first got the Sears, I got a call from
Harold's grandson, Steve Greeley. He said that he had
taken his Grandfather's Star Huckster and had restored it.
He had really wanted the Sears, but his parents wouldn't
let him take it. I told him, that if the Sears were ever for sale,
he would be the first to know.

         Around 1998, Steve called again. I told him that
it was Bev's car, and to plead his case with her. He sent
her a nice long letter, and she decided, since we were no
longer able to use it, that she would be most happy sell it to
him. When he came east from Arizona to pick it up, he was
just so happy. So were we; it was then back in the family
with a younger owner, and could be used and enjoyed for
years to come.

         Other collector cars, that we owned over a
twenty year span, included: a 1934 Lincoln V/12 sedan;
1967 Buick Sky Lark; 1963 Buick Rivera; 1965 Mustang
Convertible; various Lincoln Mark 3's; and a 1947 Dodge
Pick-up. Keeping these cars in running order was a chore,
since they were used very little. Because of sitting idle
(sometimes months in between use), each and every time
we would want to use one, it would require some repairs.
On one occasion, we wanted to take the '67 Buick to
Virginia for a car event. Before we could, it had to have

all new brake cylinders and a master cylinder installed. So, one by one, we sold all of the other collector cars, and only kept the Sears (which required very little attention), and the Auburn (which got a lot of use and didn't require much attention, either).

Between our collector cars and our modern ones, I would say that Bev and I motored over a half a million miles together. These miles were over and above all the miles that I put on the modern cars, commuting and using them for business errands.

Chapter 7:
Our Neighborhood and
Our Life Together

The East 80th Street Block Association was an organization formed in 1972, to serve, guide and better the block. Beverly joined this organization in the early 70's.

She was editor for their *Block Letter*, a position that she held, off and on, until 2007. During those years, she also served as President, Treasurer and Secretary of the organization. Beverly also wanted to see the block parties expand and grow, so she assumed the duty of Chair of Block Parties in 1987.

Beverly, on the Church steps, keeping track of the street fair

For all her work, on behalf of the Block, Beverly received the Certificate of Merit in 1978 from the Citizens Committee, City for New York Inc., in recognition of Outstanding Volunteer Service to the Community and the City of New York.

The *Block Letter*, was a newsletter for people that lived on the block, about what the Association was doing, and of any new start-up business on the block. There were about ten commercial spaces that were street level or sub-level on the block. Every time a new one started up, Bev would contact the owners, and she and I would pay them a visit. (Bev, to conduct an interview; and me, as the photographer.)

The newsletter also covered events and things happening at The Hungarian Baptist Church, on the block. The church, was a place where a lot of Block Association meetings were held. The newsletters were distributed by way of building doormen or superintendents of buildings

97

that did not have doormen.

In the early years, the annual block parties were simply for the people who lived on the block. Neighbors would set up tables on the street and sell odds and ends. The Block Association also held a White Elephant sale. This was a sale of items donated by folks on the block, from clothing to knickknacks. In the beginning, the Block Association had members who would cook in their apartments, and bring food down to the street to sell.

After a time, this practice ended, since the city would no longer allow it. So, folks would fire up the grill and sell burgers, hot dogs and soft drinks. (They still sold some baked goods, that were prepared in individual kitchens.) Along with these changes, the City required the Block Association to have a food permit each year. This was not a pleasant thing to have to do. Beverly would go downtown, to the place where these permits were issued; she'd stand in line for hours, along with city food cart venders and restaurant owners. I remember going there once, and stood on line for about an hour and a half. As I started to conclude my business, a vendor approached the other window, and the clerk closed the window. The clerk stated that it was time to close. (Civil Service workers are not always kind or caring, so you can imagine the disappointment and anguish of that person.) He was probably in line for hours, and would have to come back another day, and go through the same thing.

In 1987, Beverly wanted to advance the scope of the block parties, because she felt that more could be done to raise money, to maintain the block's planters and trees. At this point, Beverly and I would go on weekends to flea markets around the city; to Brooklyn and Long Island in search of block party vendors. We were very particular about our selections, since we were looking for quality and varied dealers. We were also very careful not to have duplicate dealers selling the same goods.

From the first year, until the end of the block parties, we would always have the block filled with vendors. We

98

also had a waiting list of other vendors that wanted to be a part of our block party; because word had spread of how well they did at this, one-block, one-day event.

When the food permits and the cooking became more effort than the Association Members cared to deal with, professional food venders were invited to sell at the block party. These vendors added considerably to the overall profits for the day, as they required large spaces in which to operate.

The street fair

Beverly also added entertainment to the Block Party. This consisted of two to three individual street musicians. She would select and hire from musicians that she had encountered on corners or in the subways. These individuals were always glad to get the work, and they were paid by funds from the block party proceeds from the day.

The members and some volunteers were very busy, for weeks before, and during the event. Some were out soliciting donations from local restaurants and other businesses, to be auctioned off (in the beginning) and raffled (later on). A raffle meant another chore, because someone had to sell tickets, which most of us did. The raffle was always a huge success, and an event that was very much looked forward to.

Two outstanding raffle ticket buyers, were Sybil and Jeff Kleinberg; neighbors and good friends who won at least one or more prizes at each Block Party Event. There were coloring parties, to color the block party posters. They would be placed in windows of local businesses and on light poles from about 74th Street to 86th Street (on four main avenues), to bring attention to the block party.

Beverly, of course, would have to handle all the calls from vendors for spaces and payments. This would start about March, and continue until just before the block party in early May. The night before, we would be out marking out the vendor spaces, and then get up early the next morning to clean the street and get the vendors on the block. After the block party ended, there was a major clean-up, to get all the debris and junk off the block; all debris had to be moved to street corners, for pick-up by New York Sanitation.

One of the last businesses to add to the success of this event was Orwasher's Bakery, at 308 East 78th street. The bakery would donate all their leftover bread on Friday evening, to be sold at the block party. It took at least four people to gather and load the bags of bread into the car. Once, on a rain-out of the block party (a dreaded thing – since Bev would start to worry about the weather about a week before), we took all the bread downtown to a homeless shelter. This, of course, was very much appreciated, since there was enough to feed the homeless for two to three days.

All of this new work and activity was not in vain, since the proceeds from the day would amount to be anywhere from $5,000 to $6,000, (as opposed to perhaps $400.00 to $600.00 in previous years). There was more than enough money to plant and maintain the flower beds, as well as deep root feeding for the trees. This work was done by Sofield Landscaping, twice a year (Spring and Fall). In addition, the Block Association paid to have new surrounds built around the flower beds. There was a planned celebration dinner, usually the following weekend, for those who put in all the effort to make the block party a success.

One other major task; taken on by the Block Association, was a wall mural on the corner of 80th Street and 2nd Avenue. The food market, that was in this space, decided to block up the windows facing 80th Street. After this was complete and whitewashed, a group of youths, led by Graffiti Artist J.J., couldn't resist the temptation of this large white wall. Every time it was whitewashed they would come and put graffiti on the wall; and, the employees of the food market would whitewash it again.

The Block Association decided to have a wall mural painted there, thinking that surely the youths would respect the art and not deface it. For this project they hired Alisa Klayman, who Bev had found by way of a restaurant owner who had a mural painted on his wall.

About the time that Alisa was ready to start the project, J. J was killed in a motorcycle accident; and as she was priming the wall to do her work, the group of youths showed up. Since they feared that J. J.'s art would be lost forever, they threatened her about covering it up. This happened for two days in a row. She assured them that she would leave a space for J.J to be remembered, and continued her work. Several of the Block Association Members would go to the corner and stay with Alisa as she worked, including Beverly.

The youths finally came to like the mural, and didn't harass her any more. When it was complete, there was a tombstone painted in the bottom corner, with R.I.P. J. J. From this time on, there was never graffiti on this wall again.

This whole episode was covered by *Our Town* and *The Daily News* papers. When it was finished, it received an Otty Award from *Our Town* with a citation that read: "Our Town Thanks You; In Recognition of playing a role in making New York City a better place to live and work."

There were many that helped make the block party and the block surroundings a success, over the years. Two main constants, in addition to Beverly, were Nell Semel and her husband Dan, from 245. Others worthy of mention are: Albert Aahronheim; Bill and Saba Pratt; Marian Rosenwasser; Charles Stevenson; May Miller; Barbra Kurzman; Jim Courtney; Nancy Gammino; Warren Goodwin; Richard and Rose Shulman; Karen Ripp; and Peggy Pugh — all from the block.

The responsibility of organizing the block parties for the last two years was given to a commercial firm that organized major block parties. For health reasons, Bev could no longer deal with the stress of dealing with all

101

the things that she had been in charge of. The Block Association received half of the proceeds, and the other half went to the promoter. The split would net each about $3000.

I asked Nell Semel to remark on Bev, she said: "Bev was a remarkable person, in who were an unusual cluster of traits. First, she had a good heart, which attracted many good friends for a lifetime. She believed in contributing her time and talent to community service. To that end, for over 30 years, she served our Block Association, throughout its existence, in many capacities: Newsletter Editor, Treasurer, President, and Block Party Chair. Not only was she community-minded, she had good ideals. She was willing to take on responsibilities and had the smarts to do a quality job. We are grateful to have known her, and considered her our very good friend and colleague".

Nell (most often referred to by Bev as Nurse Nell), was a great help to Bev. (Nell was a School Nurse, until she retired.) In my absence, she would do anything, as simple as running errands or look in on her, when she was not feeling good. Her husband, Dan, even took her to the emergency room,when necessary.

Nell & Dan Semel

In the late 70's, Beverly joined the Outdoors Club. This club, sponsored historic walks in the city, and hikes outside the city, for the more adventurous folks. Bev, of course, chose the historic walks, since hiking and mountain trails were not her 'thing,' but history surely was. She made the acquaintance of Joe and Dorothy Lovitz, who were conducting these walks at the time.

In the early 80's, Bev took over the walks, since Joe and Dorothy had reached an age when they no longer wanted to continue their role as tour leaders. One of the walks started at Columbus Circle and went up Central Park West, as far as the Dakota (a building built in the 1800's). The Dakota was so far north of the city at the time, some folks asked the builder: "You're so far out, why didn't you

102

go to the Dakotas?" (Thus, the name, Dakota.)

There were a lot of movie stars and other famous persons that lived in the Dakota over the years. John Lennon of the Beatles lived there. In fact, it was the location where he was shot down. The historic walk would continue toward the West Side to Broadway, with a lot of history to be told about the different blocks along the way. The walk included a short break at a Deli that served, as Bev said; "the best cheese cake in the city." It continued down Broadway, past other landmark buildings.

Bev's other Historic Walk started at Grand Central Station, and focused mainly on the extreme East Side and Sheeps Head Bay area, where a lot of history took place in the early years. The tour also included the historic United Nations Building Bev constantly researched and added to these walks as she found new things to add.

In a letter to the Outdoors Club, dated March 19, 1989, from Walter & Mary Granchor, Walter wrote: "Today, my wife and I participated in your city walk through mid- town East Side. The walk, led by Beverly Kimes, was an absolute delight. Beverly's in-depth knowledge of history and architecture, as well as her charming manor, made for a thoroughly interesting and enjoyable afternoon. We look forward to becoming members and participating in many more of your walks."

As you may have gathered by this time, Beverly never gave up on research. She chased it relentlessly. To her, research was like fodder to cattle...never enough. She had to give up these walks in the early 90's, due to health problems. Certainly, it was something that she enjoyed immensely, and certainly, she was sorry to have to give these up.

Sometime in the mid 80's, she joined the University of Illinois Alumni of Greater New York.. She served as recording secretary for the steering committee meetings for over a decade, until 2007. She also served on the scholarship awards committee. One of the main activities of the Alumni was to encourage area High School Graduates to attend the University of Illinois. They also organized fundraisers to fund their scholarship endeavor; they would give out scholarships to two area students that were going to the U. of I.

In 1989, she gave the Alumni group a special historic walk on the East Side, as a fundraiser for the scholarship fund. It was well attended and enjoyed by all, and Bev was given a standing ovation at the end of the walk. There weren't very many changes in the leadership of the steering committee, since there were very few willing to take on these rolls. Past presidents included: Amy Linton, Mike Murno, Brett Coffee, Kelly Belford, Hamish Defieitas. The one singular named that remained constant, and someone involved in everything, was Bruce Johnson.

Around 2000, we faced a threat that the building in which we lived would be converted from a rental to condo status. The building owner, who had been warehousing vacated apartments for several years, was finally able to use this leverage for votes for the conversion. A new Tenants' Association was formed at this time, and the members had to pay dues, so that an Attorney could be retained to review all legal matters. This new attorney, working with the owner's attorney, was engaged to ensure that the owner followed the correct procedures for the conversion. He was also retained to protect the rights of tenants, who had no intention of purchasing their apartments.

Bev joined the association as recording secretary and co-treasurer, along with Edward Maloney. She held the position until 2007. As part of the recording secretary duties, she had to inform the tenants about upcoming meetings, by posting notices in the elevators and above the mail boxes in the building. Some meetings were held in the laundry room, others at the Hungarian Church; there were quite a few. The conversion finally did take place, as we all knew it would, eventually. At least the Tenants Association had done its job to insure a proper conversion.

Some of the members of the Tenant Association, that bought their apartments, would later move over to a governing body for the apartment owners; but the balance and strength of the Tenant's Association would remain intact to protect the renters. Although at the time, Bev and I could have purchased our apartment for a good price, we elected not to. The mortgage and taxes were affordable, but we were more concerned about the monthly maintenance fees. These would be adjusted, as needed, for repairs and upkeep of the building. We knew that there were major repairs that would have to be done, over and above what the building owner had to escrow. There would be major over rides to the owners. With this in mind, we decided not to buy, but to stay on as rent-controlled tenants. I t was Bev's desire to live there until her death, and this was the one way to insure that desire. To that end; the purpose was served.

From Chicago, to New York and beyond, both Bev and I were supporters of animal shelters; we even supported Save the Whales. Bev was a very profound giver, and she sent monthly donations out to various animal shelters. One that I still support to this day is Tuffy's Place, a no kill shelter for cats. The keeper and protector, Dominic, started Tuffy's long ago, with his wife, Delores, in Larchmont, New York. We first started to help with donations in the late 90's; we named the cat that we 'adopted' from the shelter, Lilly of Larchmont (who is still alive and well.) After Dominic's wife passed away, he moved the shelter to upstate New York.

When we first got our cat, Jerry, we found out that she was feline-leukemia-positive. We didn't have her put down, (which some would say we should), and she lived a very good life, until she passed away about three years later on the bed by Bev's side. After about six months, we decided to get a pair of cats, (since pairs are happier). The two we got were tuxedo cats. Prior to going to the New York Humane Center, we had decided that these two would be named Ralph and Alice; as in the *Honeymooners*.

When we arrived there, we picked out Ralph quickly, a cute little kitty, that kept saying: "Pick me. Pick me." We were told that the only tuxedo female was an eight-year-old, and her name was Trixie. We took her, but did not change her name. We even joked about Ralph having a long affair with Trixie.

Those two cats traveled extensively with us, for what had to be over 35,000 miles. They were never put in cages, but carried out and put in the car.

Ralph and Trixie

We never had any problems with this arrangement. The only time they would let us know they had to get out, was at the end of our day's travel; they had a good sense to know when that was.

Ralph passed away at the age of eight, from bladder failure. Then, along came Oscar, also a tuxedo cat, who had been born in the wild, and rescued from under a porch. Trixie didn't care for Oscar, in the beginning, but they eventually became good friends. Trixie passed, I believe, when she was about fifteen. We got our next cat, from the pet store on 81st St. She, too,

Maggie and Oscar

was a rescued stray. Maggie was not a tuxedo cat; she was a tabby; She and Oscar got along well. Maggie was about ten when she passed away. Oscar is still with me; and I think this wild cat will be around for years to come.

On a visit to the bank one day, Bev met Henry. She called me that day and said, "Can we please adopt a dog?" Of course, I said yes. The evening that Henry's temporary caretaker was to drop him off, I made it a point to be home, as well. I was a little surprised at the size of Henry, which was something that was not discussed beforehand. Henry stood about 30 inches high, was all legs and weighed about 50 pounds. When he was let off the leash, he started running around the apartment. The cats disappeared in a hurry. I said to Bev, "I thought we were adopting a dog; he looks more like a horse!"

Bev on the study couch with Henry

Bev loved this dog dearly, and he always knew that. When Henry and I would come home, he would head directly to see Bev, and get his Beggin© Strip treat; he'd often lie on the leather couch in the study with her. When we were at the shop, he spent most of his time by her side. Henry is a mix of border collie, shepherd and husky. He's a big, and a very smart dog.

Beverly taking a break with Ralph

All of our furry friends were very good company and comfort for Beverly. If she was having a bad day, and had to be in bed, they always joined her. If she was having a slight case of writer's block, she could take time out and pet them. On some occasions, the cats would hop up on her desk, just to be petted. This little distraction would often give her a pause that would refresh her thoughts. When she was either at our shop in Matamoras, or was unable to leave the bedroom and go to the shop, Henry spent most of his day lying on her bed, with her.

When we got married, Bev became a stepmother to my three children; so, she had a family. This was good for her, since she could not have children, due to health problems. James, Jr. and Cheryl (Cheri) accepted Beverly right from the beginning. Loraine was another story. She, at first, seemed to harbor some resentment, which in time, did go away.

At age 11 or 12, Cheri wrote Beverly a note, and that said: "Dear Beverly; Thank you very much for the use of your home. Please excuse Lori, but I don't want you to feel bad, but I like you. Would you come to a play, May 22, Saturday? If you can't come, I understand. Tickets are

107

a $1.50, but I'll pay. Hope to see you there. Love always Cheri Cox; p.s. See you soon I hope."

Me with the three kids, from the left Cheryl, Jim and Loraine

In a letter to Beverly, Lori wrote: "Beverly: I have been wanting to write this letter, and I finally decided to do it. I would just like to say, I have been very cruel towards you when we have been together, and I would like to apologize for that. I have finally come to except my parents not being together. I don't like it, but I except it. Anyway, I hope you will give me a second chance. I hope we can have a good time at Action Park and at Hillcrest in the fall. I promise this year's trip will be much more pleasant. I am writing this letter for two reasons: one is because I want us to become friends, and two, because I love my father and want him to be happy. I know this letter should have been written sooner, but I am a very emotional person, and it took me time to get used to this situation. But, I know that is no excuse for my rude behavior. Well any way, I'm sorry and I hope you will forgive me. I would really like us to become friends. Sincerely, Lori. p.s. I am 15 and a good student in school, but my penmanship does lack in quality. Although I don't think that matters in this letter".

Beverly was an excellent stepmother. She was the one that made sure that birthdays and holidays were never forgotten. She was the one that took charge of getting me out shopping, whenever cards or presents were needed for birthdays and Christmas. When the kids needed money, she was right there to help; and when the two girls got married, she was also right there with financial assistance. Lori came and stayed with us for a year in New York, to attend a school for Ultrasound Technology, which Beverly and I paid for. She went to school five days a week, and would go home for the weekends with her boyfriend, Tim (who would later become her husband).

108

Bev's favorite holiday was Christmas. Before meeting me, she always went home for Christmas. She'd visit her family and, of course, dote on Cullen and Pam; giving them their much-anticipated presents. The Saurs' family moved to Northern Wisconsin in the late 70's; to God's country, as they referred to it. A few years afterward, Tom decided that he had enough of God's country. He wanted to move the family back to Wheaton, Illinois and rejoin the family business, Saurs Electric.

Sharon, however, didn't want to leave, so the couple separated. Tom returned to Illinois; Sharon still lives in God's country. Cullen also returned to Illinois and married his sweetheart, Michelle Intrepidi, from Rinelander, Wisconsin. They have one son, Thomas, and currently live in Elburn, Illinois. Pamela married William Mudra. They have two children, Grace and William; they currently live in Houston, Texas.

Bev also went home the first Christmas after we met. After Christmas, I drove to Wheaton to meet her family. Her Dad and I hit it off right away, but Grace had her reservations. She got over those in a short time, and soon afterward, I became her favorite son-in-law.

Our first Christmas Tree, Bev with little bundle of joy

We bought our first Christmas tree in 1983. This was a very special thing for both of us. It was a real tree. (The other kind would come much later, when we both were tired of the watering and clean up.) It was always my job to put the lights up in the apartment and on the tree. Bev would then

Our first Christmas, Rene du, Maurice, Beverly, and Rene

put all the trimmings on the tree and around the apartment. She enjoyed this so much, that we usually didn't take things down until late January. Starting with the first tree, and for every one after, we would buy and hang a new ornament.

Bev and me, New Year's Eve, 1982

From 1983 until 2007, we always had the kids (and later the grandkids), visit us for a Christmas dinner and gifts. These visits were sometimes on Christmas Day. The grandkids eventually numbed six. Jim and Mary Ann had two children: Brittany and James, III; Lori and Tim Reeve had three children: Nicholas, Alexia and Hailey; Cheri and Bill Redding had one child, Elizabeth.

Grand Kids, Jimmy and Brittany

Nicholas, Haile and Alexa

Elizabeth

Beverly loved to shop and wrap gifts for the grandkids. She would always put a lot of thought and effort into this, and the kids were always delighted with their presents. (Thank God, because shopping to me was a pain!) As soon as the unwrapping was done, the kids started to play with their toys in the apartment. If the weather was good, they would go out and play with the toys on the sidewalk.

The most unusual and exciting present that Bev ever found, (I don't know where she found them), were six little boxes with paper rolls inside. On each paper roll, she had attached fifty one-dollar bills. Her efforts were very well rewarded. These were the last gifts to be opened, and the kids had to open them all at once. If you could have heard the hoots and yells from the kids, as each one pulled the money out of the boxes, you would understand the joy that Bev felt. All of the grand kids loved their "Nanna Bev," as she was fondly called; and Nanna Bev surely loved them.

Another good friend of Bev's was Julie Holtzman, internationally acclaimed concert pianist, cabaret singer and teacher. We went to Julie's apartment on Central Park South for a small personal concert entitled, Julie & Jazz, Under the Stars, Overlooking Central Park.

Two notes tagged to our program said:
To Bev and Jim: A Joyous, Jazzy Healthy 98. Yours Julie "Congratulations, Bev on your "Brand New Life" It would be nice to see you again. Best J." A few years later, at Bev's request; Julie came to our apartment and did a small concert for our Block Association members.

Sometime in the 70's, Bev met Jeff Scott, who did motor sports programs on the radio. I am not sure how or where they met; it could have been at *Automobile Quarterly* or the Le Chanteclair Restaurant, since Jeff was also an amateur racecar driver. Bev became good friends with Jeff and his wife, Ann. In the late 70's, Jeff became very ill with emphysema, and was in and out of the hospital quite a bit. On weekends when Beverly was back in town, she would take Ann out for dinner and conversation, since this was a very stressful time her.

Ann and Bev would get together and play scramble. This was also good therapy for Ann, and they continued to play long after Jeff passed away. In 1991, we had dinner with Ann and her friend, John, in their home;

Ann Scott and John Quinn

and started what would become an annual tradition. Thanksgiving dinner was always excellent. Bev loved turkey and stuffing, but didn't care for the fuss of making it. (Bev did, however, make a complete turkey dinner for us for on just one occasion, Christmas 2000. It was an excellent dinner. Afterward, Bev said, "Now, I have proved to myself that I could; and that's that.") Ann and John came to our place annually, for New Years Eve, to exchange

Turkey Dinner

111

Christmas presents, have dinner and welcome in The New Year; this tradition continued until 2007.

As I mentioned in a previous chapter, Bev's idea of the purpose of the stove, was strictly for storage. She did, however, remove the cover once and made pasta with a meat sauce for our first dinner date. (She said it was the only thing she did well.) From that point on, since I liked to cook, I took over the cooking for us, and any dinner guests that joined us for a meal.

In my teens, I began learning to cook from my mother, and helping her in the kitchen (since there were six boys, before there was a girl born into the family). I improved my cooking skills when Bev bought me my first cookbook, *The 60-Minute Gourmet*, by Pierre Franey. It's a wonderful book; using his knowledge, and adjusting where I wanted, I became what I would consider to be a very good cook. You might even say, I had become an amateur chef. At any rate, I never had complaints from Bev or dinner guests.

One group of guests, worthy of mention, is the O'Rourks; Cousin, Kim; husband, Bob; and daughter, Signe. Kim and Bob were the folks Bev had lived with in New York, for a short time in the 60's. They had moved to California in the late sixties, and eventually, both became school teachers at a Catholic School. Beverly and Signe had a very special relationship, through correspondence and Signe's occasional visits to New York. Signe was trying very hard to get into acting, and of course, this had been Bev's biggest interest. Signe eventually gave up on acting, and became a teacher at the same school in which her parents taught. After Christmas, for years, they would bring a group of kids from their school to New York, to see plays and do sightseeing. On quite a few occasions, they would come to visit and have dinner with us.

The O'Rourks, from the left Kim, Bob and daughter Signe

112

When I would be away for several days, I always prepared food in portions for Bev. All she had to do was heat and eat; she really appreciated this. One of her favorite things that I made was chocolate fudge. It was from a recipe handed down from my mother. Bev really enjoyed scraping the skillet, after I had emptied the fudge onto a platter. She also enjoyed a piece of still warm fudge, as soon as it could be cut.

In the late 80's, we attended an American Bugatti Luncheon, and afterward, were invited to visit an Art Gallery by the owner. I was standing by a display case, looking at some antique toys. I had no particular interest, except enjoying how they looked. The owner came over and said in a very sly manner, "You know, Jim, these are very expensive." That statement really annoyed both Beverly and me. We went back to our apartment, got some cash and returned to the gallery; we bought two of the toys and a Mantaut print...just to prove to the owner that we could.

Those two toys sat on a shelf for over a year, before others would join them. At the time, we were not pursuing any interest in collecting toys. Sometime later, I had the occasion to go to upstate New York to do an appraisal for an estate that involved automobiles. I had finished the appraisal early, and since I could not get back to the shop in time to do anything for the day, I decided to skip the interstate roads and just meander back on secondary roads.

I came to an intersection in Bouckville, New York, and noticed a couple of antiques shops; so, I stopped to take a look. Soon, I was looking at antique toys all over the place. My interest and adrenalin started to increase rather quickly. Before I could slow down, I had purchased all the toys that my wallet, and a cash advance on a credit card, could afford.

I told Beverly about this, by phone that evening. When I got home, I said: "I guess we have become toy collectors." She said: "Well then, I think it's time to get

113

some books, and become informed about the hobby." In a very short time we had a collection of these as well.

In the beginning, we collected what appealed to each of us. Bev was quite fond of toy animals, whether they were wind up, friction or push. We had a small display case for these. (She referred to it as the "birdhouse.") My interest was mostly in cars, trucks and tractors, as well as toy buildings. After a few years, we decided to change direction, since there were just too many options in toys. Having collected quite a few items, and liking the lithographs and colors of toys made by J. Chein and Courtland Toy companies, we decided to only collect items from these two companies.

Then we had to decide what to do with the other toys. For this, we started another business: Sussex Antique Toy Store. We had now become dealers, as well as collectors. We went to toy auctions or toy shows almost every weekend. We looked for toys to add to our collection, as well as inventory for the toy shop.

We were accompanied, quite often, by our good friend, Walt Gosden. We often swapped money for purchases, since one of us usually brought more than they would be spending. Our travels would take us as far west as St. Charles, Illinois, to the Kane County Fair Ground shows. People would sell toys from the rooms of the host motel for two days prior to the show. If we weren't out of funds after those two days, we would pay for early buyer's rights on the set-up day for the show. After that, we were either broke, or didn't see a need to actually attend the show.

We would shop for toys to and from all of our annual trips to Wisconsin, to visit with Bev's family. (These annual trips ended in 2000. Bev's dad had passed away in February of 1994, and her mom passed away in late 2000.) By the time we were on our way home, every space in the car would be filled with purchases.

At one point in time, I leafed through our photo

114

albums, which contained a photo, price and location where each toy was purchased. (This was another thing that Bev organized very well.) After rounding off the cost of each entry in the albums, I said to her," Do you realize how much we have spent on toys?" Her reply to me was: "Does it matter? When one is a collector, the last concern is what you have spent, or can afford to spend, to fulfill your collecting desires." Both of us really enjoyed our new hobby. It was both recreational and a joy to us, which took us away from our everyday work duties. We chased this hobby relentlessly; always on the lookout for new things to collect or buy.

One time, we attended a Ted Maurer auction; a two-day event. First, they would auction tin litho and pressed steel toys, then plastic toys. (We previewed both before auction.) There were a lot in both types of toys, that were of interest to us for our collection and for the toy shop. After the close of the first auction, however, Bev paid for our winning bids. When we were leaving, she turned to me and said, "Well, I guess I will need to give the checking account a transfusion, since you've just broken the bank." We stayed for the second day, but my enthusiasm to bid was very low, and we did not spend much that day.

Over the years, our collection of J. Chein and Courtland toys grew to be probably the largest collection of these two toymakers in the country under one roof. We were both very proud of our collection, and when we opened our antique shop, the whole collection was there for our customers to see and enjoy.

Although the Sussex Antique Toy Shop added more work for both of us, it was really fun to have. Our ads always stood out in the toy magazines, since Bev was quite the lay-out person. We always had good items in our ads. Some folks said to us: "I don't even have to look at the header, to know that the ads are yours." We made a lot of good friends over the years, and we sold toys worldwide. On one occasion, even a collector/dealer and a good customer from Japan, came to the United States for a big auction, and made it point to visit with us. Archie and Sue

Hanson from Stevens Point, Wisconsin, were also very good friends, who collected J. Chein and other toys. When we were out West, we stopped to see them. When they came East for the Brimfield Antique Show, they always stopped to see us.

We never had a toy returned, since we only sold quality toys; and they were well represented in our ads.

Having the toy shop was quite helpful in advancing our collection. The profits were used for our purchases. We had the toy shop for over a decade, and closed it in 2002.

Bev, Henry and me, outside of Olde Scissors Factory Antiques, 2002

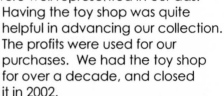

We closed our Antique Car Restoration shop on November 2, 2001. In the same location, on July 6, 2002, we opened Olde Scissors Factory Antiques. The shop was so named,

Beverly with Phil Guilhem, our friend from Alva, OK, during his visit for a Grand Classic.

The entry and check out area. Bev found the antigue brass cash register in New York; there were many offers from cutomer to buy it.

Over views of the Antique Shop; Bev's favorite room was the book room.

because one of the first businesses in that building, was the Hayes Automatic Scissors Company.

The scissors company had made and maintained equipment for all the silk mills that were in

116

the area at the time. We received a very glowing story on the front page of *Antique Trader*, written by Will Romano, entitled, *A Cut Above; Antique Heaven Found in Pennsylvania Scissors Factory*. We had to justify the building somehow, since the restoration business was no longer running, and we still owned the building.

Opening an antique shop seemed to be the ideal thing, and did prove to be a reasonably good decision.

Beverly had a really good time with this business. We took items on consignment. Bev not only enjoyed the friendship of the consignors, but also enjoyed researching items brought in or things we would buy. This gave us an idea of the history, and how the items should be priced. She was really proficient at doing this, using the Internet, which she learned to navigate quite well. The thing she enjoyed most, however, was setting up singular displays. This was a way to use her theater props experience, and her research of history for these items.

Although the shop never made much money, it did justify the space and pay our expenses. We had a person who was interested in buying the building, in 2007. We entered into a contract, and sold the building in May of that year to Peter and Tinia Larkin; they owned C.R.L Electric, an electrical contracting company. As part of the sales agreement, we were able to stay and run the antique shop until the end of the year. Realizing that this was just not in our best interest, however, we hired an auctioneer, Jeanine Tenzi, to auction off the total contents of the antique shop in September of 2007, and closed the business.

For quite some years, I had been gathering information on the building's history: who had been in the building; when they had been there; and what they did from the time the building was completed in 1925, to the time we bought it. We had framed and posted this history by the door of the shop. The last thing that Bev did, was adding C.R.L Electric to it, and hand it over to Peter.

117

One other thing left behind at the request of the Larkins, was a painting of Henry that was done by our good friend, Nicole Dreyfus. It had a caption below that said, "Henry, Official Greeter and Ambassador of Good Will, which was added by Bev. The painting hung in the front foyer of the antique shop.

I should add, that it was Henry that was responsible for the initial contact with Peter. He had been sitting out front on the sidewalk, when Peter and daughter, Caroline, were walking around the block killing time, while waiting for Tinia to be finished with a Girl Scout Parade. They stopped to pet the Henry, (who is quite pet-able), and I went out and talked with them. Peter told me that he had been looking for a building to move his business out of his house. I told him that I had about 3000 sq. feet that I could rent to him but he said he was more interested in buying than renting. He asked me to let him know, if and when, I would like to sell the building. I called him in April, and said we are ready to sell; he replied that he was ready to buy.

I believe that selling the building was a great relief, to both Beverly and me. It was becoming increasingly impossible for her to actually to spend much time in the shop. When she came out to the shop with me, she would mostly be confined to the bedroom. In part, this was due to her breathing problems, but also her lack of physical stamina. If the shop was cool and dry, she would come out front for part of the day to greet customers, write up sales, and do recordkeeping on the computer. This business required a lot of bookkeeping, since we had a lot of consignors. The individual inventory and sales records had to be maintained on a weekly basis. Over and above this, Bev was responsible for paying the consignors monthly, paying the bills for the business, paying sales taxes, and keeping the company's records; a job that she did very well.

After the building was sold, we started to pack up Bev's archives room, so that it could be moved back to our apartment in New York. In the meantime, Bev was busy clearing out the living room to accommodate the materials, and set up her new archives area. (It wouldn't matter that we no longer had a living room. Since it was used very little, the area would be ideal for her.)

We were both very happy about this move, because, at that point, all her research materials would be in one place. She would not have to travel to and from Matamoras. She could stay in a climate-controlled space, which she needed very much. (Our apartment had three air conditioners and four dehumidifiers.) She would no longer have a part in any other business. Her time could be spent entirely on doing what she loved the most: researching and writing the history of the automobile, and the individuals that made it all happen. She could also continue her job as editor for the Classic Car Club of America.

In early October, I hired a truck to pick up all the boxes and file cabinets, and bring them to New York. What we both hoped would be the greatest thing for Bev, was never to be. She had prepared the area very well, with the help of our cleaning woman, Dorota Niezgoda; she had cleaned, painted and rearranged the wall hangings. Dora, as she preferred to be called, came to America from Poland. She was a dear, and of so much help to Bev over and above her cleaning duties. She even did errands and laundry, as well as being very good company, while she was there.

Pain was Bev's worst enemy. The chronic back pain and her herpes were manageable with ice packs and her pain medications. If she were to over exert herself, however, such as engaging in physical work, the pain would be become intense and unbearable. Then, she would have to go and lay on the bed. If the pain was intense enough, she was liable to go into a comatose state, and wind up in the hospital, because of dehydration and anemia.

In October of 2007, she decided that she needed to pull the Classic Car Club, regional newsletters out from under the coffee table, and get them judged for the

119

C.C.C.A. Annual Meeting and Awards presentation. When she had finished this chore, she lugged all these out to the incinerator room to be collected by the porter. This exertion was enough to put her pain level at an unbearable level, so she went to lie down on the bed. The next day, Nell stopped by to see her about some Block-related issue. When Bev didn't answer the door, Nell let herself in, since she had a key to our apartment. When she went into the bedroom, she found Bev in a comatose state, and called her husband, Dan, to come and help to get Bev to the hospital.

This incident happened just before Thanksgiving. On Thanksgiving Day, I went to the market and bought us Thanksgiving dinner, which we shared in Bev's hospital room. She was discharged the Thursday after Thanksgiving. I went to pick her up at the hospital with her wheel chair, since it was only four blocks from the apartment, and it was much easier than trying to travel with a taxi. On the way home, she insisted that she had now seen the error of her ways, and had made a pact with our friend and neighbor, Marian Rosenwasser (who also had health problems), that the two would keep close tabs on each other.

After getting her home and settled in, she seemed to be just fine. The next morning, she was resting in bed, having breakfast and chatting with Dora, who had arrived for our weekly cleaning. When Dora left, I told Bev that I was going over to the hospital to have a chest Xray. (I was overdue to have minor surgery, but it was not life threatening. I never would have anything done to lay me up, when she needed me.) When I returned later, I found Bev curled up at the foot of the bed and completely unresponsive. I called 911, and her doctor, who said to make sure that they took her back to Lenox Hill. When the paramedics arrived, I told them that she must go to Lenox Hill, and they said that's where they were taking her.

I went in the ambulance with her to the hospital, and stayed there for about three hours, hoping that they could stabilize her, and make her conscience enough for me to talk to her before I left. She could not breath on her

120

own, so they had to insert a breathing tube into her throat, as soon as she got there. But, they were not able to stabilize her to the point where I could talk to her.

She was moved to intensive care the next day. They also had to add a feeding tube, since she could not have solid foods.   I learned that she had gotten a very bad intestinal virus when she was in the hospital before, and that was what had triggered this attack. In the beginning I asked the doctors, " What are we looking at long term?" Their reply was: "We have had cases like this before. The recovery may be lengthy, and sometimes we win and sometimes we don't."

Bev was at Lenox Hill for about four months, when they moved her to a rehabilitation hospital. This gave me hope, but it was short lived; she developed internal bleeding, and had to go back to Lenox Hill. I spoke to her doctor, Dr. Retsagi, about her condition, since it was not improving. He said that as long as her vitals are ok, we couldn't morally or ethically give up on her.

There were two important men in Bev's life at the time, other than me. One was Dr. Laszlo Retsagi, her primary care doctor. She met him in 1990, when she was admitted to the emergency room of Beth Israel North Hospital, with a kidney flare-up. Dr Retsagi had come to this country from Budapest some years prior. He had been a doctor there, as well, but had to go through medical school in the U.S. again, before he could practice medicine here. The second, was Dr. Allen M. Kaufman; Nephrology, whom Beverly started seeing prior to going on dialysis. Dr Kaufman is a leading doctor in his field, and has been selected as Doctor of The Year several times. Whenever Bev needed the attention of either one of these doctors, they were right there for her. Dr Kaufman had seen her through the dialysis, a kidney transplant and follow-up visits to monitor her, up until the day she passed away.

On several occasions when Bev needed medicine, and couldn't go out (or have someone to go to the drug

121

store for her), Dr Retsagi would drop off medications on his way home from the office. On one occasion, he came to the apartment, and took her to the emergency room.

Dr. Retsagi is fond of cars, preferring the Rolls Royce. So, there was an additional bond between him and Bev. Bev always took the latest issue of *The Classic Car* and copies of her latest books with her when going for an appointment. A note written to Bev, from Dr Retsagi, said: "Over the years, I do have a collection of the fruits of your productivity. However your most recent book with the kindest dedication tops the list." Both Dr. Kaufman and Dr. Retsagi are very dedicated and caring doctors. We all should be so lucky to have doctors like them.

Beverly stayed in intensive care for over five months. She went through endless x-rays, and scans. She also had to be put back on dialysis during this time; life was sure not pleasant for her. In the beginning, she did what she always did, dealt with it and hoped for a better day. Toward the end, she gave up. She once said to me: "Jim, please go down on the street and get something to make me go away. I don't want to be here anymore, and I want to let you get on with your life." I tried to reassure her that she would get better. By that time she couldn't speak anymore, but she plainly mouthed the words: "Bull shit; I know how I feel, and I won't get better."

I went to see Bev on Mother's day, and took some flowers and the latest get well cards. At the time, I could not get her to wake up; so, I left to do other things that needed to be done. I knew I would see her again on the

next day, Tuesday. Bev had regular visitors every day, (Nell Semel, Marian Rosenwasser, Albert Aahronheim and Bill Pratt), and quite a few occasional ones; so I knew she'd have company

In Bev's honor and memory, The Classic Car Club, created this award, which is given to the outstanding Regional Editor, at each Annual Meet of the Classic Car Club.

Dr. Retsagi, who always called and kept me up to date about Bev, called and said that she had passed away, late Monday night, May 12. This, of course was very sad news for those of us who loved and cared about her, but for her, it was best. She didn't have to suffer anymore. There was very little chance that she would have ever been a whole person again, and that would not have made her happy at all. So Heigh Ho, Bev! May God be with you. We all love and miss you.

Beverly and I had a great relationship, as husband and wife, partners and friends, for just short of 27 years. She was a great record keeper, advertising manager and bookkeeper. She kept manila files for each and every category, and if one knew the category, there was nothing that couldn't be looked up very quickly. This also applied to her historic files, as well. This was a habit that she developed from the beginning of her college years, and one that she enforced in her work for *Automobile Quarterly*. Stan Grayson once told me, that she told him: "Every new story must start with a fresh manila folder."

Bev relied on me for proofreading, helping with research, and photography, when she was doing stories in the C.C.C.A Magazine and *Automobile Quarterly*. I also helped with writing a few short technical articles for the C.C.C. A. bulletin, as well as picking cover colors for the magazine for 27 years.

From time to time, she would get calls from other historians and authors inquiring about specific information on automobiles or events. Most of the time, she was able to provide the needed information at the moment. If not; she would take the time to find the information, and either call them back or write a letter to them.

On one occasion, she got a call from Bill Rothermel, who was serving on the Car Selection Committee for The Eastern United States Concours D' Elegance. Bill posed the following question: "We have received an application for an obscure French car called a Secqueville d'Hoyeau. Have you ever heard of this car?" Bev, at the time, was

123

stumped. As Bill told me: "I stumped the Master, is all
I thought! We ended up accepting the car, and low
and behold, by the time the Concours arrived, Bev knew
everything about this damn car! I looked everywhere and
came up empty-handed, but Bev managed to somehow
to know all the details. She was amazing!"

From the time that word of Beverly's death got out,
there were endless testimonials posted on the Internet and
in all the major automotive club publications. The bottom
line on all, were pretty much the same: "We will miss you,
but you will not be forgotten."

Later in the year, I think in the fall, Don Everett
donated his Automotive Book Collection to the Saratoga
Automobile Museum, in Saratoga New York. This museum
is fairly new, and was very grateful to have this collection
donated to them. At the time, they didn't have much
space for a library. Since then, however, they have
acquired another building across the way. They have
also gotten several grants to renovate the building, and
this building will be the library when completed.

Don and Mary Everett traveled to Saratoga, after
the books were received, to dedicate them. In his remarks
he said "A sad event occurred in May. Beverly Rae Kimes
was taken home by her heavenly Father. She is suffering no
more pain. Her loving husband, Jim, can take comfort in
knowing she was loved and admired by so many friends
and readers of her books. Her memory will always be kept
alive though them. She was a dear friend of ours for more
than 40 years. It was her ideal that we give the books to
the Saratoga Auto Museum, which we are happy to do.
We, therefore, wish to dedicate all of the books we have
donated to the museum library to the memory of Beverly
Rae Kimes. Thank You."   After packing up and sending
Bev's automotive book library to the Classic Car Museum,
I donated duplicates and other books and magazines to
the Saratoga Museum as well.

Beverly knew Don, long before me, but Don and
Mary became good friends of mine, as well. They always

stopped by our shop for a visit, during their annual trips to Connecticut, to visit with their daughter, Wendy, and to take their granddaughter trick-or-treating at Halloween. Since they no longer can make this trip, due to Don's illness with Parkinson's, I have been to see them in Michigan twice in the last couple of years.

When I made the decision to do this biography, I really didn't know much about Bev's early life, since she didn't discuss this much. She had talked about a few singular points in time, but nothing in detail. I am forever grateful to her; for saving all the things she did save. Without these, this book would not have been possible; at least in the sense that I wanted it to be. Others suggested that they would be interested in doing a biography about Bev, but their ideal was more concerned about her career. I rejected these, since this was not what I had in mind.

Many people knew Beverly from different sectors of her life, but none knew the whole aspect of how and why she became the person she was. She really did not engage in conversations about herself. Beverly deserves this, and it's my hope that those who read this book will have better understanding of just who Beverly Rae Kimes really was.

On August 17, 2009, Bev's Birthday, I delivered her ashes, desk, chair, and a few of her favorite items, to be placed on the desk, to the C.C.C.A Museum at Hickory Corners, Michigan; these were to be placed by her automotive book collection.

The thing that would have made me the happiest would have been for her to recover, and be able to enjoy her work in new surroundings in New York. I loved her very much, and I miss her every day. For all the good she did for mankind, God bless her. May she always be remembered as simply Bev... a girl on the go.

What If?

One of the joys of owning a Classic, of course, is driving it — whether it be on a Nation; CARavan, a regional tour, or just with a bunch of friends. Not only do we have a wonderful time, but we get an inkling of what it was like to travel in the Classic era. But only an inkling, of course, because our cars may be classic but this era is not.

Which got me to thinking. What was it really like to travel during the Classic Era? Two thoughts immediately sprang to mind. One was W. C. Fields, who was probably among this nation's more relentless motorists during the Twenties and Thirties. Each winter in New York City, he would pile himself and a bunch of friends into his Cadillac and other classic limousines and head for the warmer weather in Florida. But, unfortunately, since they also piled a healthy quantity of booze to fortify themselves on the way, no one involved — least of all W. C. — could remember much of what happened en route. Which means, that would be a story hard to tell.

So another thought sprang to mind: the classic Frank Capra film 1934, *It Happened One Night,* which probably many of you recall. Remember how Clark Gable infuriated the T-shirt Industry by not wearing one. Remember how cute Claudette Colbert looked in Gable's pajamas, and how clever she was — not to mention what great legs she had — in proving a better hitchhiker as they trekked from Miami to New York. And, of course, that blanket called the "walls of Jericho" in the various tourist cabins they spent their nights in, which eventually came tumbling down, right before "The End" flashed on the screen.

By the Classic Era, the automobile had already begun remaking society in its image. The plank swung between two running boards, which had sufficed as a bed during the early era of caravanning, had already been replaced by cabin courts such as those Clark and Claudette visited in *It Happened One Night*. And, already there were roadside hot dog stands and diners. Granted, America was still a long way from the Hiltons, Holiday Inns and Hyatts we're used to today, but travel had become relatively civilized by then. So I thought it might be more fun tonight to talk about what it was like to travel when things were not quite so civilized.

So the subject of what follows is What If... What if our Classic had been built at the turn of the century. What would touring have been like then? Now, granted, I am putting Classic Era engineering into a period earlier by a couple of decades. Some of the cars I'll be mentioning would grow up to be Classics; others would not even make it to the Classic Era. But regardless of how much more sophisticated automobiles became after 1925, they would have had to endure turn-of-the-century conditions had they been around then. Which would have made for some interesting motoring trips. So, this talk is kind of a tribute to those daring travelers who first proved that driving could be fun, indeed that traveling substantial distances by automobile was possible at all.

The most substantial distance, of course, was coast to coast. In 1903, according to a Department of Agriculture study, less than 7% of all the roads in the united States were "improved," which was the department's term meaning surfaced at all, with stones, gravel, shells, planking, whatever. Thus it was not surprising that. in a San Francisco bar one day that year, when two men were chatting about wonders of horseless carriages, one of them prophesied that nobody would ever drive a car across the country. The other man bet $50 that he could do it in three months. He was a physician named H. Nelson Jackson, who would ever after be immortalized as the Mad Doctor. The other man immediately accepted the $50 bet.

Among all professional groups in America, doctors were the first to enthusiastically embrace the horseless age. Though there were a few naysayers; virtually everyone at that time who had taken the Hippocratic oath, was convinced that driving was good for you. Cranking an engine was efficient for daily calisthenics, for example; sunlight in an open car helped anemia; and the open air was good for consumption, asthma and chronic bronchitis. Moreover, as one doctor of the era commented, and I quote, "The jolting which occurs when a motorcar is driven as fair speed conduces to healthy agitation that acts on the liver. This aids their performance of their functions."

If there are any doctors in our audience tonight, perhaps they would agree with this assessment. And I suspect they would also have had the foolhardy spirit of adventure, like Mad Doctor Jackson, that would have persuaded them to try what no man had tried before. Actually, pride entered into Jackson's decision, too. Having made the $50 bar bet, he couldn't figure out how to get out of it gracefully.

The next few days he searched for somebody crazy enough to join him in the adventure, and finally found S. K. Crocker, a young mechanic from Tacoma, who in turn found a 1904 Winton that had recently been bought by a Wells Fargo agent. The car was purchased — and they began to get ready.

Of course, we put a good deal of thought into packing before a trip in our Classics. But back in 1903 one had a lot more things to have to think about. Thus, before taking off from San Francisco, the newly purchased two-passenger Winton was laden down with waterproofed sleeping bags, rubber macintoshes, leather coats, canvas bag for water, a firemen's axe and a shovel, a compass, a telescope, a set of machinist's tools and spare parts, a vice and a pair of jack screws, a block and tackle — and some pretty heavy artillery. By that I mean a rifle, a shotgun, and two .38 revolvers. The firearms were to use to secure game for food in sparsely populated areas, and also for protection against outlaws. Remember the west was still wild and wooly then. A couple of fishing rods were added, too. The gasoline tank held 12 gallons; another 20 were strapped on behind, and room was found somewhere for an extra five gallons of oil. Two spare tires were fitted over the hood. All in all, the car was not what you would call a pretty sight.

Thusly equipped, the pair took off from San Francisco on May 23, electing for a northern route, which would take them up into Oregon, then across Idaho into Wyoming. Barely had they made it into Oregon, however, than they were stalled for three days waiting for the new tires to arrive, for which they had wired Goodrich in San Francisco. The original rubber on their car was ruined already. For a while, the intrepid duo obviously knew they couldn't make it all they way across the country like that. It's hard to imagine today, what it would have been like to travel through mountains where there were no roads; but these stalwarts were trying.

There were compensations. In every Rocky Mountain town, they approached the saloons emptied immediately as sheepherders, ranchers, traders, cowboys and Indians crowded into the street to see the extraordinary sight of an automobile. Probably Jackson and Crocker didn't have to pay for a drink all the way across the West. But the novelty of their trek had its drawbacks, too. On one occasion, a redheaded woman on a white horse gave them directions that took them 25 miles out of their way. It seemed she wanted them to pass her house, because no one in her family had ever seen a car before. Indeed, in some of the hinterlands, people had never even heard of an automobile before, and some thought the Winton was a small railroad locomotive that had somehow derailed and was searching madly for its tracks.

Gasoline was usually available in the small western towns, but at often exorbitant prices—$5.25 for a five-gallon tin in one place. (Which was a lot of money in 1903.) With Idaho, came heavy rain and mud. In one day, the block and tackle had to be used 17 times, and the car made a grand total of 6 miles. Shortly thereafter, Dr. Jackson took on a mascot, a bull terrier he rescued from a dogfight

whom he nicknamed Bud. Bud quickly proved himself
a good traveler, too, and in arid sections was provided
a pair of goggles to protect his eyes from alkali dust. I've
seen a great picture of him with the goggles on,
incidentally.

The going was relatively fun for a while, until someplace
in Wyoming, the trio — two men, one dog — found
themselves completely deserted. No villages, so streams
to fish in, nothing flying overhead for dinner. This was the
bad part. A good supply of drinking water remained in the
water bag, alkali water could be used for the car, but after
36 hours without food, Jackson and Crocker began looking
at Bud in a new light. Fortunately for the dog, the two men
didn't have the heart to make their mascot their dinner,
and decided they would all three starve together, if
necessary. Luckily, just hours after making this humanitarian
decision, a shepherd was spotted — and dinner followed.

It was in a town in Wyoming, that Dr. Jackson learned he
had competition in this mad drive of his. Two men in a
Packard were already traveling east through Nevada.
Two others, in an Oldsmobile, were about to leave San
Francisco. Both were headed for New York. Now, in
addition, the Winton Company, in Cleveland, was aware
of what Jackson was trying to do, and because both the
Packard and the Oldsmobile treks were manufacturer-
sponsored, Alexander Winton quickly became the sponsor
of men and dog in the car he manufactured, sending
them free part as quickly as they were needed.

And, with the head start, the Winton did ,of course, reach
New York City first. Driving from sunrise until it was dark each
night, they motored on, reaching Manhattan on July 26, by
which time the Packard was in Nebraska, the Oldsmobile in
Colorado. The Winton had traveled about 6,000 miles in 63
days. Jackson had gained a dog that became a lifelong
pet, but had lost 20 pounds and spent $5,000 on the trip.
As for the $50 bet which started the whole thing; would
you believe the other guy never paid up? But it did give
Dr. Jackson a great line to deliver at cocktail parties for the
rest of his life.

131

Meanwhile, let's pick up those other intrepid automobilists who had started across the continent after Dr. Jackson. First, the Model F Packard nicknamed, Old Pacific, which had left San Francisco on June 20. Its crew consisted of Packard Company man, Tom Fetch and Marius Krarup, Editor of *The Automobile;* which was a terrific idea, since it guaranteed great publicity all across the country. The Packard's motoring gear was similar to the Winton's, with a few substitutions and additions: a stout shovel, two 6x20' canvas strips and some heavy logging chains for mud and sand, It also included rather more complete instrumentation than the Winton had been provided: a compass, thermometer, barometer, gradiometer and extra cyclometer. Plus, an extra axle, a large umbrella and the requisite .38.

Early transcontinental runs were always started from the Pacific coast. Logically, it was thought best to get through the worst, first. There were no roads or bridges west of Denver, except for those built by the railroads. Nor were there guides, signs or route numbers of any kind. The only map available was that of the Union Pacific. Very quickly, Fetch discovered that following what looked like a road, wasn't a good idea, since it usually ended up on somebody's front yard. So, he stuck to open country and his compass. Not often did he ask directions either, since most folks out that way had never traveled further than a day's drive in a horse and buggy. Perhaps, too, he had heard of Dr. Jackson's earlier encounter with the redhead on horseback. The Packard's was a far more organized trek than the Winton's had been — with gasoline shipped ahead by rail to the various destinations — but, Fetch and Krarup shared many of the Winton trekker's zany adventures, too. They arrived in Carson City, for example, shortly after a murder had been committed, and everybody in town, including the sheriff, left the scene of the crime to get a gander at the car. In another town, they arrived on a Sunday morning and left the church pastor preaching to rows of empty pews, as the entire congregation ran outside for a look.

Plunging down mountains was scary, needless to say, since brake technology was rather naïve at the time. Afterwards, Flech liked to tell of holding on for dear life all the way down, and at the bottom "spitting on the brake band to watch it bounce off." In Colorado, rain made the alkali road like soap, which made steering impossible and resulted in the Packard sliding its way through much of the state, with one of the men behind the wheel, the other outside the car to guide it in the right direction. By mid-August the Packard had reached Tarrytown, New York, where it was joined by a huge caravan of 200 cars for the final trek into Manhattan. The reporter for *Motor Age*, wrote, "The machine was bending all the 8mph speed limits going into New York City." The Packard arrived there on August 21, beating the Winton's time across the country by two days.

The Oldsmobile which had started trekking east on July, broke no speed records. Partly because the little curved dash runabout had half the numbers of cylinders, and about half the horsepower of its rivals... and partly because the intrepid duo aboard — L.L. Whitman and Eugene Hammond — had a good many more misadventures. They needed 73 days to cross the continent, 10 more than the Winton, 12 more than the Packard. But Whitman had a super sense of humor, which no doubt, helped considerably throughout the trek, and his retelling of it made for super reading.

There were the good times; like the string of rainbow trout they caught in one stream, the fish virtually leaping out of the water, he said, probably to get a good look at the car. Lake Tahoe was gorgeous, but in the grandeur of the Sierras, as Whitman wrote, "Mother Nature cast aside her natural dignity to wantonly loop-the-loop." In Reno, they prepared themselves for the desert, but not, alas, for whatever it was that pierced their radiator midway. This left them without water in the middle of nowhere. There was nothing for them to do, but abandon the car and strike out for the railroad, which they figured to be about 8 miles away as the crow files (though as Whitman said, probably no intelligent crow had ever flown in that country.)

133

Floundering through an ocean of sagebrush, they came upon a section house, which itself had been abandoned — no people, no water. Pulling their belts a notch tighter, they trudged on along the ties, until an inhabited rail station was reached about 15 miles further. After filling their canteens with water, they flagged a midnight train west, which left them off in vicinity of where they thought they had left the car. There they took to foot again, until coming upon a settlement where they secured the services of a horse, lunch and more water, and set out into the sagebrush to find their poor little deserted Olds. It was right where they left it, of course, car thievery not being the practiced art it would soon be.

Neither the Packard, not the Winton, had endured anything like this. It rained six times in five days. There were 10 inches of rainfall in 24 hours. They tied up for nine days waiting for the rains to subside, and when they didn't, decided to flounder on through it. "The Missouri spread itself with blatant egotism," Whitman wrote — a great line that I wish I had written myself. Council Bluffs needed only a few gondolas and the palace of the Doges to be come Venice. "We took to a hill whenever we sighted one," Whitman wrote, "shook ourselves like water panels, baled out the machine and splashed on." He rather wished there had been a mermaid somewhere in his family tree. But, they made it to New York City, finally, "from Golden Gate to Hell Gate," as Whitman would title his memoir. And, miraculously, he and Eugene Hammond were still friends, although he admitted 5,000 miles of palship from coast to coast was sometimes a strain. "To bridal couples who may come to contemplate it as a transcontinental honeymoon," he allowed, "I offer a vigorous disparagement."

But disparagement notwithstanding, Whitman had soon hit the trail again — in 1904 from San Francisco to New York with Franklin and a fellow named C.S. Carris. Again, adventures abounded. In a small settlement called Wadsworth in the midst of a Nevada desert, the station agent warned them they had better get out of there pretty quick or they'd be likely to be held up by road agents.

134

Seems 20 murders had been committed with in two miles of the place in the two weeks previous. Five dollars in your pocket could be the price of your life in those parts, and in broad daylight around Wadsworth, you could see murdered unfortunates being carried out into the sagebrush to be left for coyotes. Needless to say, it was pedal to the metal for Whitman, as he beat a hasty retreat. The sight of bleached bones in the desert just motivated the Franklin drivers to go faster.

Part of this trek was spent on railroad tracks, riding over the ties providing more comfortable travel in really bad spots. They did meet some covered wagons laden with immigrants headed west. But mostly, it was a solitary journey. A washout near Fort Collins would have been a delaying disaster, except for a team of horses and a amendable driver on the other side of the stream. Well, the driver was amenable anyway after Whitman, with water up to the floor of his car and the Franklin steadily sinking deeper, shouted across, "Fifty cents for fifty feet" (which was a very good teamster wage in those days).

Whitman arrived in New York City just shy of 33 days after leaving San Francisco, which cut the old transcontinental record in half. How much of this was due to the fear of God being put into the travelers at Wadsworth is problematical.

But three years later, in 1907, Whitman took another Franklin, this time a six, from coast to coast again. And again, bumped over railway ties for a goodly pace in the Far West. He waltzed and slid and, as he said, "swung partners" all through Nebraska. Occasionally he landed in ditches and sometimes plunged into barbed wire fences. Alternately he roasted, shivered, fasted and thirsted mightily; he plunged in, dug out and came in under the wire in New York City in just a little over 15 days.

Some in the audience tonight may note that, thus far in this discourse, it appears motoring in those days was strictly a masculine sport. And, it's true that there was largely a macho aspect to the whole thing. Prevailing consensus was that if women weren't smart enough to vote, they surely didn't have any business on a trip that required one to have his wits about him at all times. But, in 1908, Fred Trinkle had the nerve to take his wife, Florence, along when they trekked the country in their Brush Runabout. They each carried a .33, incidentally. But, the silk face mask that Florence cleverly devised to ward off the swarm of gnats in early morning drives, so offended her husband, that to please him, Florence removed it before motoring into town. I guess you could say that Flo had come partway, Baby.

This sort of bowing to masculine sensibilities wasn't necessary for Alice Ramsey, however. She was the wife of a Hackensack lawyer who was later Republican congressman from New Jersey, and when she went off cross country in 1909 in a Maxwell, she took only women along: her two sister-in-laws and another female friend. Alice, Nettie, Maggie, and Hermione not only made it from Broadway to the Golden Gate, they did it in a blaze of publicity that probably no other transcontinentalist had thus far enjoyed. The first women to drive from coast to coast all alone — my, how scandalous.

But scandalous, too, was the condition of roads in the United States during that period. In 1904, the American Automobile Association had sponsored a run for New York to St. Louis. St. Louis was that site of the World's Fair, and where the National Good Road Convention was then being held. Among those attending the Convention, incidentally, was President Theodore Roosevelt. Although the transcontinental treks of the Winton, Packard and Oldsmobile had provided tremendous publicity for their manufacturers, more importantly, they pointed up the desperate need of good roads for the coming automotive age. Among the motorists who joined in the caravans from New York to St. Louis, was millionaire sportsman Charles J. Glidden, who inaugurated the renowned Glidden Tours with a trek through New England in 1905.

The Glidden became an annual event, of close to two weeks' duration, covering 1,000 or more miles, and with about 125 participants during the good years. In other

136

words, from the solitary drives across the country to prove a point, motoring by now had collectivized into a kind of precursor to our club tours. Most definitely, a point was still being made in these runs — specifically, calling attention to the crying need for good roads. And for those manufacturers who entered cars, in addition to those owners who simply participated on their own, points were hoped to be made regarding the durability of their product. Still, these early tours were meant to be somewhat enjoyable too, and to illustrate the pleasures that real motoring provided. For this reason, sections of the country that required one to pack a .38 were not toured, obviously. Indeed, New England was the location of the first two Gliddens. Not until 1907 was the starting point pushed as far west as Cleveland. For 1908 the site returned to New England. For 1909, it wended from Detroit all the way to Kansas City, which was then pretty up-to-date.

But, the fact that the Gliddens did not have to be pistol packing, should not infer the tours were lacking in arduousness. Consider the 1910 tour, which wended its way from Cincinnati through Kentucky, Tennessee, Arkansas, Oklahoma, Kansas and Iowa to Chicago. On the second day's run from Louisville to Nashville, local natives informed then tourists that the road to Bowling Green had been built 150 years before, and had not been fixed since. The fourth day from Sheffield to Memphis included a stretch through a field of stumps just high enough to strip off mufflers, bend radius and torsion rods and play havoc with fenders. On day five, from Memphis to Little Rock, one of the cars broke its axle in an Alabama swamp, another sunk in a bog, another had its differential shot to pieces, yet another its steering gears stripped. Day six, from Little Rock to Hot Springs, saw one car which had broken a spring the day before, break an axle and give up the fight. Another had the entire right side of its frame done in. About a third of the cars that had started this Glidden, were now out of it.

Day eight, from Texarkana to Dallas, found friendly farmers tossing bags filled with peaches and plums into the cars as they passed by — which in a way, demonstrated how far

137

the automobile had come, considering what farmers had routinely thrown at automobiles just a few years before. Day nine, from Dallas to Lawton, brought deep sand, hot winds and temperatures so high that leaves on the corn had turned brown. Day twelve, from Wichita to Kansas City, was equally dramatic. As a driver in a Moline complained, "One minute we were enveloped in dust, and in five minutes we were putting on rubber coats and mud chains, only to be roasted by burning sun soon after." More than 100 cars had started in this Glidden. Just 11 finished.

I daresay that everyone in the audience tonight has noticed that, thus far, I have not mentioned any tours in the Delaware Valley Region. There is a reason. Thus far, there had been none. From 1903 to 1907, there were eleven trips made by automobilists from coast to coast, and every one of those automobilists elected to hug the roads around Lake Erie and take the Upstate New York route, dropping down around Albany for the final stretch into New York City. And, there was a reason. The roads around here were abominable. Indeed, one intrepid automobilist of the period said that no road conditions in the wild and wooly west, except maybe for the Bitter Creek District in Wyoming, the abandoned trails around the head of the Great Salt Lake in Utah and the heavy roads of the Carson Sink County in Nevada, were as bad as the roads around here. Even the Gliddens, for the most part, bypassed this region.

In 1910, however, four men and an E-M-F were sent on a path finding excursion in this area prior to the Munsey Tour. In the report they wrote of their venture afterwards, they recounted the march of General Washington's army from Easton to Wilkes-Barre in 1778, when this section was virtually impenetrable; the soldiers cutting their way through thick underbrush, many of them dying of exertion and fatigue, but leaving behind some sort of road through the wilderness in the process. That road was now not much better than it had been in 1778, the E-M-F drivers said.

"Primitive" was the precise word they used. The rocky waterbreaks and gullies and washouts gave the car and its occupants the most severe shaking they had received since starting out from Philadelphia. So hard was the going, that the headlamps were shaken loose, the trunk rack fell off and they almost lost their windshield. Nonetheless, they persevered. Indeed, they elected not to have lunch, because they were determined to finish the 90-mile trip that day. And, they succeeded. Sometime later, wined and dined at the governor's mansion in Harrisburg, the pathfinders were assured that convicts were hard at work making better roads.

A couple of years later, some progress obviously had been made, because the Premier Automobile Company sponsored yet another pathfinding tour of the region, with somewhat more positive results. On the run from Hanover to Westminster and into Baltimore, the road conditions were ideal. From Baltimore to Washington, the entire road was macadam except for a stretch of a half-dozen miles outside the District of Columbia which was miserable. From Washington to Rockville and Frederick, the roads were poor again, consisting of red loam which, when wet, became very slippery. But, the pathfinders noticed convicts working roadside, and figured help was on the way. In Pennsylvania, things were even better. There remained the thank-you-ma'ams in some areas for which the state was notorious. But in large measures, the motorists rolled through the rolling hills of eastern Pennsylvania. From Harrisburg, they detoured back to Mt. Joy and Marietta, crossing the Susquehanna at Columbia. That stretch, and the one from there to York and Hanover, were quite good, but as the tourists noted acidly, "not what they should have been considering the $15 paid for tolls" that day.

Interestingly, the roads through the Alleghenies were those most enjoyed by the pathfinders, because although going up might take time, they could coast down and have a breather.

In their final report, the Premier drivers concluded that this was fine country to tour in, the breathtaking scenery being worth the occasional problems. And, I quote: "while the roads in places are pretty bad, there is nothing to cause loss of life or even serious inconvenience if, in the event of being disabled, you have assistance of another cars at hand."

Summing up, in 1911, the Premier drivers concluded that the four great essentials for successful touring in the area were:

> A slow pace and constant watch-out for high centers and road obstructions
> A reliable car
> A cheerful disposition
> A group of cars traveling with you

It's kind of interesting how things have not changed much since 1911. Touring in our classics, it certainly does help to have a reliable car as well as a group of cars touring with you. Admittedly, road technology has improved immeasurable in the last 75 years, but not all roads are always good today, either. Interestingly, though, it no longer costs $15 in tolls to get through this area. Still, a cheerful disposition is always recommended. So, with that advice from 1911, I wish you Happy Classic Motoring in the Delaware Valley Region.

Appendix B

(This article appeared in the Gamma Chapter News Journal on U. of I. campus, and serves as testimony of how Bev earned her reputation as a "Girl On The Go")

Gamma's Girl on the Go

By Mary Ann Haun

Beverly Rae Kimes, or Bev as she is known to her sisters and friend, has been appointed General Manager of the university Theatre, which is one of the four major activities on the University of Illinois campus. Bev's job includes coordinating the work of the senior staff, the junior department managers, the sophomore assistant managers, and the 250 crewmembers. She will also server as the student representative on the Theatre Board, which is composed of professors in literature, theatre and speech. Bev received her position through appointment from the members of this board.

As a freshman, she started at the bottom as a crewmember; then she became a sophomore assistant; a junior department manager in charge of properties, staging and construction; and finally, she reached the highest student position in theatre. Bev, a junior in journalism, is from Wheaton, Illinois. Not only is she active on campus, but also she maintains a high scholastic average and plans to go into foreign correspondence or diplomatic work after graduation.

Bev is as active in the house, as she is on campus. She has served as editor, rush chairman, and Sheequon chairman. Outside of her theatre activities, the list of Bev's organizations and honors seems unbelievable.

She is a member of Shi-Ai, a sophomore woman's honor sorority in which she served as vice-president; Torch, a junior woman's activity; Theta Sigma Phi, a national woman's journalism honor society; Mask and Bauble; a theatre honor organization; National Collegiate Players, a national organization to raise the standard of college theatre; Illini Union major chairman of Cinema Internationale, a group devoted to bringing foreign films to campus; Illini Forum of the Illini Forensic Association, a weekly radio program where current and contemporary subjects of interest are discussed by student; and a finalist in the Houston memorial Speech Award, given each year in honor of a distinguished alumna, Alfred Houston.

As an underclassman, Bev was a freshman and sophomore manager of the Illio, the campus yearbook, property chairman of the Spring Musical, Oklahoma; and a sophomore manager of Starcourse, an organization that brings cultural and entertaining groups to campus.

Gamma Chapter is very proud of her outstanding achievements at the university, and still marvels at their girl-on-the-go, Beverly Kimes.

Awards and Citations

1978 — The Citizens Committee City for New York City Inc. Certificate of Merit, In recognition of Outstanding Volunteer Service to the Community and the, City of New York

1978 — Cugnot Award, The Nash Story, for outstanding research

1983 — The Thomas McKean Award for most significant original research, My Two Lives

1984 — Cugnot Award, Outstanding book of 1983, My two Lives — Race Driver to Restaurateur, with Rene Dreyfus

1985 — I.A.M.A. Moto Award, Outstanding Achievement in Automotive Journalism

1985 — The Thomas Mckean Award, for most significant original research

1986 — Cugnot Award, Outstanding book of 1985, The Standard Catalog of American Cars, with Henry Austin Clark Jr.

1986 — Society of Automotive History, Friend of Automotive History Award. In recognition of her dedication and significant contributions to the cause of Automotive History

1987 — The Thomas McKean Award, The Star and the Laurel, a Centennial History Daimler, Mercedes and Benz, for most significant original research

1987 — Cugnot Award, The Star and the Laurel, Outstanding book of 1986.

1988 — Certificate of Honorary Membership, Antique Automobile Club of America

1991 — Classic Car Club of America, Citation for Distinguished Service (This award given on rare occasions, singles out those persons — who though exceptional leadership, vivid imagination and rare organizational ability — inspire their associates in a concerted effort towards the fulfillment of worthwhile club goals.)

1993 — Automotive Hall of Fame, Distinguished Service Citation (This award was presented to Beverly for being one of the nation's foremost automotive historians; for encyclopedic research into American automotive history, scholarly works about Ford, Chevrolet, Packard and other motorcars; and her dedication to the preservation of Automotive history. Beverly is the only female historian and journalist in the Automotive Hall of Fame.)

1994 — S.A.H. Carl Benz Award, Ken Purdy, King of the Road, an article in Automobile Quarterly

1995 — The Burn Prevention Foundation, Concours d! Elegance, for Distinguished and Meritorious Service

1996 — I.A.M.A, Moto Award for Outstanding Achievement in International Media

1999 — Carl Benz Award, "Austie" Henry Austin Clark Jr., an article in Automobile Quarterly

2000 — Auburn, Cord, Duesenberg Club, Woman of the Year

2001 — C.C.C.A. Spirit of St. Louis Region: "In appreciation for your many achievements as a gifted scholar, noted historian, renowned author, prolific editor, eminent lecturer and above all immeasurable friend."

2002 — I.A.M.A. Moto Award, Category: Best of the Best of Magazines

2002 — Cugnot Award, Outstanding book in the English Language, The Classic Era. (The reason for the change to the English Language was due to the S.A.H. awarding honors to other languages.)

2002 — Thomas McKean Award for most significant original research

2002 — Certificate of Appreciation from S.A.H. Past President, LeRoy Cole

2002 — The Classic Car Club of America, at their 50th Annual Meeting, presented to Beverly with a bound album with 69 Testimonial Letters (from all walks of her life). This recognition was spearheaded by C.C.C. A. Member, George Tissin of Scottsdale, AZ.

2004 — Carl Benz Award, The Story Behind The Marmon, for anoutstanding article in Automobile Quarterly

2005 — I.A.M.A. Lifetime Achievement Award

2006 — Cugnot Award for Best Book, Pioneers, Engineers and Scoundrels, The Dawn of the Automobile in America

2008 — George L. Weiss Memorial Trophy for Meritorious Service rendered to Packard. This Award is presented by Packard's International Club. (They held this award for a few years, because they wanted Beverly to be present at an Annual Meeting to receive it. Unfortunately, her health would not enable her to travel. In the early part of 2008, after several phone conversations with Dwight Heinmuller about her health, he decided to mail the award to me. Beverly did get to see the Award, before she passed away.)

Books Written or Edited, as a Freelance

My Two Lives, Race Driver to Restaurateur, with Rene Dreyfus

The Standard Catalog of American Cars 1806 to 1942, with Henry Austin Clark

The Star and the Laurel, The Centennial History of Daimler, Mercedes and Benz

The Classic Car, for The Classic Car Club of America

The Classic Era, for The Classic Car Club

Pioneers, Engineers and Scoundrels, The Dawn of The Automobile in America

Marr, Buick's Amazing Engineer

Pebble Beach, Concours d! Elegance, The First 50 Years

Speed, Style and Grace, The Ralph Lauren Collection, with Winston Scott Goodfellow

Otis Chandler: The Pursuit of Uncommon Excellence, with Randy Leffingwell (Bev also wrote A Tribute to Otis for the Inaugural Rocky Mountain Concours d! Elegance.

Edited, Walter Dorwin Teague, Biography, Industrial Designer (In addition to being an industrial engineer, Teague was most noted for developing the entire body designs for the Mamon Automobile, V/16 models of the early 1930's.)

Edited, W.F. Millikens Equations of Motion, a Biography. (Bill started his early years, after graduating from M.I.T. in aircraft, and later, started a company with son, Doug, dealing with automobile aerodynamics and stabilization.)

146

Beverly was a contributing writer to several publications, Star, The Official Publication for the Mercedes Club, Life Magazine, Car and Track, Wheels, the official Publication of the Detroit Public Library, Automotive Collection Bulletin, and various others. One of my favorites was an article in Special Interest Auto, August 1987, SIA #100. It's a story about the 1970 Plymouth Super Bird, featuring Richard (King) Petty and is written in a Shakespearian Theme.

Bev also did all the Tablet writings in the early years for The Miles Collier, Automobile Museum in Naples Florida.

Acknowledgements

I would like to thank Bobbie'dine Rodda, of Glendale California, better known as "Miss Information," who was a true caring friend. She always sent Bev get-well cards that would arrive each each day, every time Bev was ill. She was always a good source for photos when Bev needed

them for the Classic Car Club events. Thank you Bobbie'dine for everything.

My deepest thanks to Phil Gillian, a dear and faithful friend, who helped to proofread this manuscript as it progressed, and for making the T-shirt honoring Bev's memory.

I would also like to thank the OutSource Marketing Group, Inc., Kutztown for their help in the design and editing of this book.

Bobby'dine wearing a T-Shirt, honoring Beverly. The shirt was made by Phil Guilhem of Ava, OK.